WEB SITES
BUILT
TO LAST

WEB SITES BUILT TO LAST

Lessons from Leading Sites for Surviving and Prospering on the Internet

By
Marc Kramer

Adams Media Corporation
Avon, Massachusetts

Published by Adams Media Corporation
57 Littlefield Street, Avon, MA 02322. U.S.A.
www.adamsmedia.com

ISBN: 1-58062-373-5

Printed in Canada

J I H G F E D C B A

Library of Congress Cataloging-in-Publication Data
Kramer, Marc.
Web sites built to last / Marc Kramer.
p.   cm.
ISBN 1-58062-373-5
1. Electronic commerce. 2. Web sites.
3. Business enterprises--Computer network resources.
I. Title.
HF5548.32 .K733 2002
658.8'4--dc21
                                    2002010013

This publication is designed to provide accurate and authoritative information
with regard to the subject matter covered. It is sold with the understanding that
the publisher is not engaged in rendering legal, accounting, or other professional
advice. If legal advice or other expert assistance is required, the services of a
competent professional person should be sought.

—— From a *Declaration of Principles* jointly adopted by a
Committee of the American Bar Association
and a Committee of Publishers and Associations

This book is available for quantity discounts for bulk purchases.
For information call 1-800-872-5627.

Visit our home page at *www.adamsmedia.com*

Contents

Dedication and Acknowledgments vii

Preface ix

Chapter 1: Developing a Business Plan 1

Chapter 2: Developing a Web Site Plan 11

Chapter 3: Developing a Marketing Plan 31

Chapter 4: Selecting the Right Consultants 53

Chapter 5: Web Site Hosting 65

Chapter 6: Strategies and Implementation
for Long-Term Success 81

Chapter 7: Retail Gifts 95

Chapter 8: Financial Services: B2C 111

Chapter 9: Human Resource Service Sites 127

Chapter 10: Entertainment 143

Chapter 11: B2B Market Sites 159

Chapter 12: Financial Services 171

Chapter 13: Business Services/Products 187

Chapter 14: Government Commerce 203

Chapter 15: Future Predictions 215

Appendix A: Sample Business Plan 229

Index 261

Dedication

All of my books are dedicated to my wife and daughters, because more often than not, I am an absentee husband and father, even when my physical presence is sitting at the dinner table. They have been very understanding.

Acknowledgments

In every book I write I always thank my wife Jackie because without her support I couldn't succeed. I want to thank my daughters, Ariel and Sydney, who motivate me to write these books and who make my life interesting.

I much appreciate all of the executives who consented to let me interview them for this book, and my clients for giving me a great education that gave me the experience to write this book. I would like to thank Gary Samartino, Gail Jones, Debra Goldring, Mike Perry, Ellen Weber, and Mark Talaba for reviewing sections of this book and giving me their feedback.

The following people obtained access for me with their corporate leaders, who are featured in this book: Tara Burgess, Francine Coulter, Marylou Gross, Jennifer Richardson, Ryan Rosenberg, and Kathleen McGrogan. I appreciate their help immensely.

Finally, I want to thank Bob Adams, president of Adams Media, and Jere Calmes, my former editor, for allowing me to write this book.

Preface

Two years ago, the Internet was so hot and stock prices were through the roof. Then one day, Alan Greenspan, chairman of the Federal Reserve, made a comment during a United States Senate hearing about "irrational exuberance" and the walls came tumbling down.

People who had been so high on the promise of the Internet dumped their stocks so fast that stocks weren't just dropping a couple of dollars, they were dropping $10, $20, $30, and as much as $50 in a day. Players like John Doerr—a partner at revered Kleiner Perkins, the 800-pound venture capital gorilla who had claimed there was a new world order in business and made hundreds of millions taking companies public—started telling us from the safety of their Palm Springs winter homes that they were wrong. Yes, the Internet is a breakthrough technology, but it didn't cause the earthshaking paradigm shift that Wall Street and Silicon Valley gurus predicted.

I believe the opportunity for establishing a successful Internet venture is greater now than it was at the height of the frenzy. The technology is better, there are more users, companies have people dedicated to building internal and external Web sites to do everything from internal communication to buying and selling products and services.

What has happened to the Internet in the beginning of this new millennium reminds me of what happened to biotechnology in 1990. Scientist from companies and universities were leaving to start revolutionary drug products. Billions of dollars were invested in hundreds of companies. The gold rush for this sector was almost identical to the Internet gold rush that followed.

Early investors made a lot of money and people who came to the party late made the early investors a lot of money by buying their stocks at artificially high prices. Unfortunately, the latecomers lost a lot of money. People were forgetting that it typically takes $500 million to take a drug from development to getting an approval from the Food and Drug Administration and from start to finish takes about ten years.

Ten years after that initial gold rush, biotechnology has been coming back into vogue as a good investment from a venture capital and public investment perspective. Drugs are starting to be approved and substantial businesses are being built at companies like Amegen, Cephalon, Centocor (which was acquired by Johnson & Johnson), and Genentech.

The Internet's in better shape than biotechnology because the cost of development is going down and the usage is going up. I doubt you will see the investor frenzy that we saw in the beginning, but I predict healthy growth. I will give you eight reasons why selling and servicing clients over the Internet has more profit potential now than at the end of the last century.

1. **Ease of Use.** A few years ago, I bought gifts on Red Envelope, a pure Internet transaction. The site was difficult to navigate and the time it took to go from one screen to another was long enough for me to run to the store and buy it. Today Web site programming is better and practically everyone has a faster modem or some form of high-speed connection.

2. **Wireless Use.** I was on a train with a friend who needed to order flowers for his mother. Not only was he stuck on a train, but it was after 8 P.M., when florists are closed. He attached his phone to his computer and bought an arrangement at *www.1800 flowers.com.*

3. **Confirmation Capability.** Two years ago, aside from Amazon and a few others who developed in-house e-mail customer response, you weren't sure if your purchase went through and when it would be shipped. Today, there is plenty of off-the-shelf customer response and management software for small e-commerce sites to use.

4. **Improved Security.** In the early 1990s, people were afraid that their credit card information would be snatched out of cyber

space. The number of American adults using credit cards to purchase goods and services online more than doubled between 1998 and 1999, according to research by Cyber Dialogue. By the third quarter of 1999, 19.2 million adults used their credit cards to make online transactions, compared to 9.3 million in 1998 and only 4.9 million in 1997.

5. **Increased Business Purchasing.** According to the Gartner Group, companies will spend $433 billion on the Web in 2001 compared to $200 billion plus in 2000. Why is everyone purchasing more? There are more common standards of programming that make it easier and controllable. "Merchants competing in the online environment see a great opportunity to reduce their accounts receivable and collection expenses, while also providing value-added services to corporate clients," said Cory Gaines, VP for Emerging Markets at Visa USA.

6. **Increased Consumer Purchasing**. More than half of the U.S. adult population has made a purchase online, taking e-commerce from a dot-com novelty to the mainstream, according to a survey by Nielsen//NetRatings and Harris Interactive. This will only increase as, unfortunately, Americans become afraid of going to malls and consequently use the Internet to make purchases.

7. **Low Cost of Web Site Development.** With all of the off-the-shelf products available, anyone can have a quality first generation site built for less than $100,000.

8. **Decreasing Acquisition Cost.** Marketing online, according to Eagle Marketing, is one-tenth of the price of direct mail, five times more efficient, and will bring customer acquisition costs down.

If people were getting rid of their Internet connections like my father got rid of his CB, then I would agree it was fad, but do you know of anyone who is closing his or her Internet account? I know the Internet is taking hold because my wife, an avowed anti-technologist, pays the bills on our Central American home through the Internet and buys all of our far-flung relatives gifts through the Internet.

The companies that are going to make it are going to have one or more of the following ten characteristics:

1. **High Margins.** The best businesses to get into are high-margin businesses, which allow management to make mistakes and take risks. A company like eBay has very high margins because they don't take possession of anything.

2. **High Volume.** If you don't have high margins, then you better do a volume business. eBay has the luxury of being both high margin and high volume. The companies that fit mostly likely in this category are online stock broker firms like E*Trade and online travel such as Orbitz and Priceline. Much to everyone's surprise, Priceline is profitable.

3. **Low Customer Acquisition Cost.** The largest cost for any business, regardless of whether it's online or offline, is customer acquisition. Companies that can privately label their services and leverage other people's contacts and members are going to be winners. There is an online affinity bank called The Bancorp, which is headquartered in Delaware. They develop partnerships with affinity groups such as universities and national clubs and provide their students and members with online banking capability. The affinity group markets them to their members, basically eliminating their marketing cost.

4. **Unique Offering.** The products or services being sold are unique and have a large enough population to create a successful business. I like a company called AskDrTech (*www.askdrtech.com*), which provides an online service to help anyone with a computer problem. Everyone has computer problems and this site provides answers in two ways: querying a database and going through the site and contacting a live human being.

5. **Good Money Management.** You have to respect money and believe that whatever money you raise needs to be marshaled out smartly. The good managers don't put their companies in Class "A" office facilities; they look for the cheapest space. They buy everything at a discount and they don't add people until absolutely necessary.

6. **Niche Opportunity.** The companies that focus on a particular group that isn't being overserved have a terrific opportunity. There is a company called InvestorForce, *www.investor force.com*, which is featured in this book. They provide the information about money managers to allow pension fund managers to evaluate them.

7. **Low-Maintenance Cost.** If you have to keep rebuilding the site every year and support a large number of programmers, you won't be around for long. You need to be able to maintain the site with a small group of people. There is a site called Bizlaunch (*www.bizlaunch.net*), which provides individuals with a twenty-four-step process to start a new business. This company aggregates other people's services to support their customer base. Their only cost is updating content.

8. **Repeat Users.** Because customer acquisition costs is one of the most expensive parts of running any business and especially an online business, businesses that attract repeat buyers lower their customer acquisition cost and build a profitable business over-time. Take a look at WebStakes (*www.webstakes.com*), an online game site, which provides a variety of new games every day. Web Stakes is building up a tremendous database to market other people's products and services.

9. **Creative but Sensible Management.** Too many venture capital firms are rushing to put financial types into leadership positions thinking that they will hold the line on spending. I am all for putting a person who is good at stretching a dollar in the chief

operating officer role, but I definitely think the companies that will succeed over time will have marketing people at the top. Marketing people are usually strategic thinkers who see and come up with creative ways to build brand equity and attract customers. The top person has to be visionary and the second in command needs to figure out how to make that vision a reality without running the car off the road and out of the race. The management team at popular real estate and home improvement site Home Store (*www.homestore.com*) presents a good example.

10. **Customer Support.** The companies that fail to provide outstanding customer support have no chance of making it. How many times have you gone to a site and can't find a telephone number or e-mail address to contact, or even if you find them no one in the company contacts you back for days? I firmly believe Amazon (*www.amazon.com*) has done everything right in terms of providing quality customer support and a pleasurable experience.

You probably noticed that I didn't mention cash as one of the criteria. I think everyone realizes that is a given. What I hope you take from this book is what it takes to plan, develop, and build a business that will either be a stand-alone profitable company, increase sales in a traditional bricks and mortar company, or build a significant enough following that a larger, more well financed company will want to buy it.

This book is organized to take the reader through the steps of building a quality Web site business, regardless of how much money you have to invest. The book takes you through:

- Developing a business plan for the Web site
- Developing a sales and marketing plan
- Developing a proposal for Web developers to respond to
- Selecting the right hardware to host your site
- Selecting the appropriate consultants
- Companies and business models I believe will be successful

No business can actually last forever. Businesses are built to take advantage of an opportunity or need at a particular time and place in society's evolution. The Internet is part of that evolution and those who read this book will appreciate the hard work, planning, and creativity required to survive and thrive.

Chapter 1
Developing a Business Plan

WHAT IS A WEB SITE THAT IS BUILT TO LAST? Building a quality Web site that works is only part of the answer; the most important part is building a business model that will leverage the medium and will make money. Over the last five years, I have worked with many public companies and entrepreneurial startups that were leveraging the Internet to do one of three things:

1. Enhance their existing business
2. Protect the territory of an existing business
3. Create a new business to compete with an existing bricks-and-mortar business

Bricks and Mortar Hubris

Bricks-and-mortar companies that were early adopters of the Internet are now past the point of putting up a "brochure" online. They are creating destinations for clients and prospects to come to in order to buy services and products and receive customer service on existing services and products. The problem with many pre-Internet businesses is

1

that they don't look at the Internet like pure Internet businesses do. They think of the Internet as if it were another communications technology like a computer or fax machine.

The companies who "get it" realize their existing model will be rendered obsolete and at a minimum will lose market share to companies embracing the Internet. Therefore, they have to provide their customers and prospects with a Web site that enhances the value of the business relationship. Old-line traditional businesses like Mack Trucks and VWR Scientific (a reseller of medical-related products to pharmaceutical companies, research organizations, and hospitals) were early adopters and continue to use the medium.

What I have found is that many of these companies make the mistake of assigning the head of marketing to work in conjunction with the chief information officer (CIO) to develop and implement a Web strategy. The strategy basically is an extension of their existing marketing and customer initiatives. Once the site is up, they hire or move someone from marketing or information systems (IT) to manage the site. They don't put in place a true leader who has a passion for developing and improving their Internet initiative to the point that it becomes a stand-alone business or at the very least a strong division.

20 Questions Focusing on Long-Term Success

There are twenty questions every traditional company should ask itself before it builds a Web site:

1. Do we want to increase revenues?
2. Do we want to decrease expenses?
3. Do we want to accomplish both?
4. Do we want to promote our products and services and let our existing sales distribution network close the deals?

5. Do we want to eliminate our existing sales distribution network and have every purchase be serviced by our Web site?

6. How will the site be marketed so customers and prospects know it exists?

7. If the company is selling products, will users be able to buy all of the company's products through the site or only a select few?

8. How much will the site cost to build?

9. How much will it cost to maintain?

10. Will we outsource the building of the site to an outside firm?

11. Will we outsource the maintaining of the site to an outside firm?

12. Will we host the site ourselves or outsource hosting?

13. Who will be responsible for deciding the day-to-day content changes of the Web site?

14. Will the site be marketed independently or will it be forced to piggyback on the company's existing marketing budget, and who will be responsible for marketing the site?

15. Will the site rely on existing IT personnel for product upgrades or will it have its own team?

16. Will the site have its own technology budget?

17. Will the site try to meet or exceed what its competitors have developed?

18. What is the approval process for future enhancements to the site?

19. How will the site be measured in terms of meeting overall corporate goals?

20. Will the person in charge of the site report to the company CEO or will he be two or three levels down the corporate food chain?

Pure Plays

Internet entrepreneurs often forget that they are building a business and not just a technological work of art. The stock market has sent a strong message to pure dot.com companies, and that is you have to focus on keeping your expenses low and attaining profits within a three-year period. I have had many Internet entrepreneurs ask me to develop a request for proposal for a new Web site before they develop a business plan. When I ask to see their business plan, they tell me either that they are working on one or that one isn't necessary for an Internet business.

Anyone who is going to develop an Internet business needs to ask herself the following ten questions:

1. Will consumers and/or companies buy what I am selling through the Internet?
2. Will the Internet give me a competitive advantage?
3. Is there a successful existing bricks-and-mortar business model selling the same types of products and services I plan to offer?
4. Will I be able to offer an advantage in price or service over traditional businesses?
5. Are traditional businesses offering the same products and services I am and, if so, what will my competitive advantage be?
6. What kind of functionality and how many products will I offer?
7. Can I tell a compelling enough story to raise capital?
8. Can I recruit people who can make my business a success?
9. Do I know enough about the market I am focusing on to build a profitable business?
10. How much money will it cost to build my business before I am cash flow positive?

In today's business climate, you shouldn't even consider starting a business without having developed a business plan to test your assumptions about your concept. Shacks are built without plans. Strong, enduring homes with a minimal amount of problems require architectural and construction plans, because selecting the wrong layout and ground and building materials could result in a house that falls on top of you after you move in. Well, a business plan is the architectural blueprint for your business.

A business plan should be a realistic view of the expectations and long-term objectives for a business. It provides the framework within which it must operate and, ultimately, succeed or fail. For management or entrepreneurs seeking external support, the plan is the most important road map that they are ever likely to produce, as it is key to focusing the company and to raising capital. Preparation of a comprehensive plan will not guarantee success in raising funds or mobilizing support, but lack of a sound plan will—almost certainly—ensure failure.

The ultimate goal of a business plan is to develop a road map that will lead to financial success. In today's financial climate, any Internet-related company that isn't focused on being profitable within a three-year time period would not be able to raise money. As this book is being written, there are companies such as Bizbuyer and Mother Nature, who have returned $35 million and $13 million, respectively, to their investors because their plans couldn't substantiate a profit in an acceptable time period.

A formal business plan serves four critical functions.

- It helps management or an entrepreneur to clarify, focus, and research their business's or project's development and prospects
- It provides a thought-out logical framework within which a business can develop and pursue business strategies over the next three to five years
- It serves as a basis for discussion with potential internal and external investors
- It offers a benchmark against which actual performance can be measured and reviewed

There are basically twelve sections to a business plan, and they are as follows.

1. *Executive summary.* This is the most important section of the business plan because it summarizes the business model and provides potential and current employees and investors with the problem you are solving, the revenue opportunity, and what it will take to build the business. This section, which should be two to three pages in length, includes the following subheadings:

    - Problem—Define the problem in a paragraph or two.
    - Solution—Explain your solution in a paragraph.
    - Market—Provide information on the total size of your target market.
    - Marketing/Sales—Describe your strategy for building sales.
    - Revenue—Describe how you will make money.
    - Competition—Describe your competitors.
    - Competitive Advantage—Give reasons why your product/ service is better than the competition's.
    - Management—Provide a one-sentence description of the key executives.
    - Capital Requirement—Produce a paragraph on how much money you need and what you need it for.

2. *Description of the business.* A one- to two-page description of the product(s) and service(s) you are offering.

3. *Company objectives.* A one-page description of the goals the company has set in the area of number of new customers, gross revenue, profit margin, client retention, and revenue per employee.

4. *Market for the business.* A two- to four-page description of the size of the market. A good place to find sources for tracking research information to support your plan are: *www.ceoexpress.com, www.cyberatlas.com, www.census.gov,* and *www.sba.gov*

5. *Marketing strategy.* A page or two on the individuals you are marketing to, the tactics you plan to use to reach them, and the entities and tools you plan to use to execute your marketing plan

and build visibility with your potential users.

6. *Sales strategy.* A page or two on how you plan to sell your product/service to your customer. This will focus on developing and implementing direct sales force, strategic partners, joint venture partners, and affiliate programs.

7. *Revenue streams.* A page or two of descriptions of each revenue stream.

8. *Retention plan.* Rarely have I worked with a company that has given a lot of thought to how it plans to retain its customers once it gets them. This section, which is a page or two in length, should provide detail into such tactics as developing user advisory boards, having an outside person interview your customers, developing customer newsletters, and so forth.

9. *Competition.* Most of my clients either tell me that they have no competitors, or they list anyone who could be a competitor and go overboard on the number of competitors they actually have. This section should be four to five pages and include a strengths-and-weaknesses analysis on who your competitors are and how you measure up to and are different from them.

10. *Management/board.* A two- to three-page description of each executive in the organization and each board member. The descriptions of each person should be no more than two paragraphs and contain only information that is relevant to the business opportunity.

11. *Launch plan.* A one- to two-page spreadsheet that details how you plan to roll out the site and build the business over the first twelve months.

12. *Financials.* One-year cash flow statement and five-year financial projections.

Note: Financials are just as important to develop for an existing business developing a Web site as they are for a pure Internet company.

It is important for a traditional company to not only know what its expenses are, but to figure out how its Web initiative can either stand on its own or provide income lead generation or expense reduction that management can point to as a way of determining success or failure.

Just as no two businesses are alike, so also with business plans. Nonetheless, most plans follow a well-tried and tested structure and offer general advice on preparing a plan that is universally applicable.

The following suggestions will help you create a quality plan.

- The most important and difficult sections to prepare relate to marketing and sales, as these can make or break not only the business plan, but also the business itself!
- The financial projections are likely to be straightforward, but decide on a sensible level of detail regarding the time horizon.

Microsoft Office comes with financial spreadsheets and financial modeling options. Two other good software packages designed to assist with business plan writing are Plan A (from Internet Capital Bulletin Board, Inc.) and Plan Write (from Business Resource Software, Inc.). Both packages ask the user a series of questions, the answers to which the user types in. When the user finishes answering all of the questions, a formal business plan with financials is provided.

- When drafting the plan, be positive but realistic about the business's prospects, and explicitly recognize and respond honestly to shortcomings and risks.
- The management section of the plan is crucial—it should demonstrate the management's experience, balance, ability, and commitment. Remember that the fate of the company is not in the product, but in the management team.
- Avoid unnecessary jargon, economize on words, and use short, crisp sentences and bullet points. Always check to make sure all

words are spelled correctly. When there are significant issues, break the text into numbered paragraphs or sections, and relegate detail to appendices.

- Get a qualified outsider to review your plan in draft form. Be prepared to adjust the plan in the light of the reviewer's comments.
- Support market and sales projections with market research. Ensure that there is a direct relationship between market analysis, sales forecasts, and financial projections. Assess competitors' positions and possible responses realistically.
- Restrict the level of detail on product specifications and technical issues.
- Be realistic about sales expectations, profit margins, and funding requirements.
- Ensure that financial ratios are in line with industry norms. Do not underestimate the cost and time required for product development, market entry, securing external support, or raising capital. Consider the possibility of the halve-double rule—halve the sales projections and double the cost and time required.
- When looking for external equity, be realistic about the value of the business, risks involved, and possible returns, and be sure to indicate possible exit mechanisms. Put yourself in the shoes of an investor and remember the golden rule—he who has the gold makes all the rules.

Sample Plan

A regional gift store chain in the Midwest decided that it had to cannibalize its existing business by putting its products on the Internet. The president of the company believed that using the Internet was less expensive and had far greater reach than opening new bricks-and-mortar stores. She decided that a business plan needed to be written as if the company were launching a new company. She did this for three reasons.

Outside validation: She wanted an outside firm to validate whether selling her products on the Internet made sense. She believed that if venture capitalists showed interest in investing, then her thinking would be validated.

Potential funding source: She wanted to send the plan to venture capitalists to give her company another financing option.

Management buy-in: She wanted to make sure her management team took the new venture seriously and would embrace her vision.

In the appendix of the book is a sample business plan.

Chapter Summary

Before you even begin to write the first check for your new venture or to take your existing business and put it online, take the time to write a business plan. There are several reasons why you should write a business plan.

1. A business plan will provide you insights into whether your concept should be sold through the Internet.
2. A business plan will force you to look closely at your competitors and see if you can differentiate yourself.
3. A business plan will force you to think through how you will market and sell your product/service.
4. A business plan will help you develop a discipline that will enhance your chances of success.

You will save yourself a lot of money if you think your concept through first, regardless of whether it is a successful bricks-and-mortar business.

Chapter 2
Developing a Web Site Plan

ONCE YOU DETERMINE THERE IS A MARKET for your Internet concept, you need to develop a technology plan on how you are going to build the site.

All too often, companies make the mistake of calling in Web site developers and handing them a simple description of what they want to build. Many of my clients believe if they show an experienced developer one or more Web sites that match their concept, the developer will be able to give them a price.

Building a Successful Web Site Plan

There are four steps to developing a good Web site plan:

1. Decide who is responsible day-to-day for the Web site.
2. Develop a request for proposal.
3. Develop a criterion and list of developers to interview.
4. Develop a list of hosting services to interview.

Web Site Leader

Someone has to be responsible on a day-to-day basis for the Web site. In the case of a bricks-and-mortar business that is using the Internet as another means to provide products and services to its prospects and clients, the person should have the following authority and expertise:

- Content decision-making capability
- Direct access to the president of the company
- Shared authority on technology implementation
- Expertise in marketing
- Understanding of the company's overall strategic business goals

Developing a Request for Proposal

Before you launch your venture and begin to solicit investors, make sure you understand how long it will take and how much it will cost to build a quality Web site that you can add on to and won't have to scrap after one year. I had an international client that hired one of the largest Web development companies in the world. My client didn't develop a plan to give to developers that mapped out exactly what information it wanted to give to prospects and customers, and how that information would be extracted and integrated with its current information systems.

By the time the project was complete—to the tune of $400,000—the chairman/CEO of the company fired the developer and the internal people who were responsible for development of the site. He realized the site was a failure when customers called and wrote to him about problems accessing important information and the difficulty in navigating the site. He then had his new CIO and vice president of marketing work together with myself and outside developers to come up with a new plan. The new site, which will be much more robust and user friendly than the old site, will cost almost half of what the old site cost to develop.

Develop a Criterion and List of Developers to Interview

A common mistake companies make when developing a Web site is to call either the largest companies because they have read in business and trade publications that XYZ company is large and has done work for certain well-known companies, or small developers thinking they can save money and hold out the "future work opportunities" carrot to extract a lower price and quicker development time. Before hiring a developer, you need to develop a written plan for what you want. The plan should focus on four tasks:

1. Find a developer that understands the market you are selling to. For example, if you are a pharmaceutical company developing a Web site for doctors, you want to hire a developer who doesn't have to be educated on what type of computer systems doctors use to access the Internet, and what their preferences are in terms of on-site technology such as the use of Flash and frames.

2. Find a developer that is within driving time of the person in charge of the project. The Internet is a great communication tool for interacting with customers who are spread out geographically, but it has been my experience that when developing a complex site, it is good to be able to meet in person with your developers.

3. Ask the developer who your project manager will be and what his or her credentials are. One of my clients was in the process of hiring a nationally known developer, which I actually knew a lot about. I asked my client who the project manager in charge was. My client said it had met with a group of seasoned people but hadn't been told who would oversee the project. I advised the client that before signing anything, he should find out who was running the project and what experience that person had in developing projects for my client's particular industry, and whether that person had implemented technology similar to what my client was looking to

13

use. Make sure that the developer isn't trying to pawn off the third team project manager. Also make sure that under no circumstances can the project manager be removed from the project without your approval.

4. Develop a spreadsheet that lists the criteria that you are going to measure each potential developer by. On your side of the table should be the heads of operations, marketing, information systems, customer retention, and financial, and the internal person in charge of working with the developers.

Don't be in such a rush to develop your site that you make bad choices that eat up a lot of money, lose time to market, and ultimately cost more than taking one's time and making an educated choice.

Develop a List of Hosting Services to Interview

If you haven't developed a Web site before and bought hosting services, you need to have someone guide you through the process, especially if you are developing an e-commerce site. There are three questions you should ask any hosting service:

1. *How often do you upgrade your hardware and software?* This is important because you want to make sure that your site can use the newest technologies and graphics upgrades, and that the chance of the site's going down through lack of proper maintenance is minimized.

2. *Do you have a mirrored service in another building in another geographic area?* Four years ago, I was visiting MCI's hosting farm in Pentagon City outside of Washington, D.C. The computers that hosted the Academy Awards, Procter & Gamble, and others were on one of the top floors. As we were getting a tour, I asked the manager of the facility where the backup facility was, and he

smiled and replied that a backup facility wasn't needed because the building was fireproof. All I could think of was, didn't this guy watch the movie *Towering Inferno*? I wonder if P&G knew this or assumed that MCI, now WorldCom, had a backup facility. Don't assume anything, ask!

3. *What is the skill level of your technicians, and is someone on-site 24/7, including holidays?* A client of mine had his site go down on Thanksgiving and it cost him over $10,000 in orders. Another client had a problem with its site and the hosting company had to call someone in from Oracle to fix the problem, because its people weren't trained on Oracle.

Chapter 5 will discuss the topic of hosting in greater detail, but this will give you a sense of what you need to ask.

Elements of a Proposal

Don't delude yourself into thinking that your plan will be perfect. Developing a proposal to give to developers is a great first step. It provides insights into what you think you want and need. Good developers will be able to take your plan and provide feedback that will improve your site and possibly save you money.

There are six parts to a good proposal: mission, content, user description, site technology, internal technology, and site map.

Mission

The mission of your Web site should describe what your company and the user will get out of the site. The mission of Dell Computer's Web site is to allow buyers to save time and money by building their own computer. The value to Dell is that they develop a one-on-one relationship with the buyer, and they don't have to build computers that may not meet the customer's needs.

Content

What type of information will the user find on the site? Content will range from basic company information to descriptions of products and services to press releases to white papers about the company's industry.

User Description

The developers need to know if the end user is a consumer with a traditional 28.8 or 56K modem, or a corporate user with high-speed access. This will give the developer insights into the type of graphics and audio and video streaming technology the user will have access to.

Site Technology

All site content is written in a word processor or text editor and converted to HTML or XML. Professional developers use Go Live and Macromedia's Web authoring tools. Developers need to know whether there will be databases to which users will have access. Will those databases be accessible to everyone, or will they be password protected? What database program was used to develop those databases and were all of the databases that users will have access to developed in one common language? Do you plan to use video and audio streaming, and how many people do you anticipate using video and audio at one time? The developers need to know all of this to determine what type of professionals to include in the site's development team.

Internal Technology

Developers need to know what type of hardware and operating systems your databases and content reside on, in case they have to extract information or build links to information that resides on internal computers. They also need to know if you plan to host your Web site internally or outsource it.

Site Map

There are two types of site maps that need to be developed. One is a spreadsheet that includes: names for each section and subsection, descriptions of each section, and the type of software and technology required to access the information for each section. The developers need to know who, on the client's team, is responsible for what. Finally, the developers need to know what the company projects in terms of the number of pages each section and subsection will require.

The other site map looks like an architectural plan. It includes boxes with the names of each section and subsection mentioned in the spreadsheet site map plan, and arrows between the boxes indicating how the sections and subsections are linked to one another.

Sample Proposal

The proposal you develop should be labeled "Draft." This is because you will be revising the information in the plan based on the discussions, feedback, and questions you get from developers. What follows is a sample request for proposal for Web site developers to review.

Cocci.com Request for Proposal

Contact Person: Marc Kramer
610-873-6978
marc@kramercommunications.com

Description of the Company: Cocci.com is an e-commerce company that will provide 200 choices of birthday cards and 10,000 choices of children's gifts that are under $25. The company will be marketed to mothers and grandmothers.

Budget: Client wants a lasting quality solution and will pay a fair price.

Operating Environment: The company is new. The technology will be mostly Microsoft and possibly some Oracle related to the databases. No accounting package has been selected, so the company is open to recommendations.

Order Fulfillment: Fosdick.

Technical Requirement: Below is an overview of the type of information we will supply to Web site developers. The focus will be on developing a graphically inviting home page that is quickly downloaded and utilizing off-the-shelf products for electronic commerce, customer service, and security.

Technical Capabilities
User Section

1,000 products scalable to 10,000

Ability to e-mail customer and sender when gift is purchased

Ability to view products

Ability to add other products to shopping cart

Ability to create and send a business letter using Kramer form letters—200 scalable to 2,000 choices

Ability to create and send a video e-mail

Ability to have customer electronic wallet so key information doesn't have to be reloaded

Ability to turn off graphics

Ability to hear background music. This music would be embedded in the Web site

No frames

Date reminder capability—birthday, graduation, employment anniversary, customer renewal

Search engine

Free mail box (Delta3 Communication) that translates from e-mail to voice mail

Technical Capabilities (continued)
Business Operations

Connect warehouse and fulfillment to Cocci.com accounting system

Inventory adjustments on sister sites accessing same products must be connected

Develop an accounting system providing information on buyer, buyer's geography, individual product sales, and shipping cost

Provide credit card capability and money transfer directly to Cocci.com account

Ability to know the number of hits

Ability to know which items were clicked on

Ability to use live person to take orders and sell other products

Ability to personalize a sender thank-you for buying from Cocci.com

Ability to maintain and change site once it is up—adding products and content

Preference toward off-the-shelf solutions and minimal customized building

Develop backup system—mirror site and backend capabilities with another server

Note: Affiliates will need access to an Extranet that is password protected and that allows them to see the commissions they have earned and to find out about contests we will be running. I don't know if you want to include that in this phase or not.

Site Plan
Company

Section	Content	No. of pgs.	Programming
Background/Mission	History of the company	1	Static
Executive Contacts	Top four execs bio and e-mail/general phone number	1	Static/e-mail link
Sales Contacts	Sales contacts by region/e-mail/tele.	1	Static/e-mail link
Service Contacts	Head of service e-mail	1	Static/e-mail link
Partnership Opportunities	Details on how to join affiliates program link to sales	1	Static/e-mail link
Return Policy	Explanation of return policy	1	Static

Occasions

Section	Content	No. of pgs.	Programming
Anniversary	10 card choices and links to suggested gifts	10	Small pics/link to full pics
Birthday	10 card choices and links to suggested gifts	10	Small pics/link to full pics
Business Thank-You	10 card choices and links to suggested gifts	10	Small pics/link to full pics
Friend Thank-You	10 card choices and links to suggested gifts	10	Small pics/link to full pics
Grade School Graduation	10 card choices and links to suggested gifts	10	Small pics/link to full pics
Sales Honors	10 card choices and links to suggested gifts	10	Small pics/link to full pics

Occasions, *continued*

Section	Content	No. of pgs.	Programming
Corporate Promotional Gift	10 card choices and links to suggested gifts	10	Small pics/link to full pics
Religious Event	10 card choices and links to suggested gifts	10	Small pics/link to full pics
Make Your Own	Ability to choose clip art and write card	10	Small pics/link to full pics

Product Categories

Section	Content	No. of pgs.	Programming
Sports	Baseball, basketball, football, golf, hockey, and soccer	10	Pic/static-ecom
Movies	Posters, pens, and other novelties	10	Pic/static-ecom
Personal Care	Cosmetics, fans, and sunglasses	10	Pic/static-ecom
Business Supplies	Calculators, folders, paperweights, and pens	10	Pic/static-ecom
School Supplies	Calculators, folders, lunch boxes, and pens	10	Pic/static-ecom
Religious	Mezuzahs, crosses, Buddhas, and yarmulkes	10	Pic/static-ecom
Toys	Matchbox sets, models, race cars, and train sets	10	Pic/static-ecom
Games	Games for all ages	10	Pic/static-ecom
Apparel	Gloves, T-shirts, shorts, and sweatshirts	10	Pic/static-ecom
Linen	Pillowcases, sheets, and towels	10	Pic/static-ecom

Gift Genie

Helps users go through selection process

Section	Content	No. of pgs.	Programming
Select card by occasion	Search by occasion with suggestions	1	Links to Occasion selections
Select a gift	Search by Occasion or Product Category	1	Link to Occasion/Product
Pick wrapping paper	Pictures of 10 types of paper	1	Pic/static-ecom
Fill out recipient address	Fill out once and information is stored	1	E-comm link to database
Fill out sender address	Fill out once and information is stored	1	Cyber wallet

Site Assistant

Section	Content	No. of pgs.	Programming
Search Engine	Ability to search site for cards and gifts	1	SQL
Site Map	Ability to link from site map	1	Text links

Total 213

Planning Advice

When you read the interviews in the chapters on the various industries, you will notice that one thing most business leaders underestimate is the amount of planning, time, and cost that goes into developing a quality Web site. Below is an interview with Jim Letts, who has personally been involved with developing some of the most well-known content and e-commerce Web sites (go to *www.usinteractive.com*) in world industries as diverse as banking, entertainment, health care, and travel.

Insights from the Trenches

Jim Letts is the chief technology officer for one of the largest Web site developers in the world, US Interactive, which has offices all over the world. Letts, who has a degree in electrical engineering from Yale and a master's degree in business from the Wharton School at the University of Pennsylvania, has been in the multimedia/Internet business for almost a decade. Few people in the world have worked on the variety of projects that Letts has worked and consulted on.

What are technical issues you are concerned about in an extensive content-oriented Web site?

The four different areas are:

- *Link management.* This is the process by which you make sure links from one part of the content to another part of the content are correct and valid. The challenge with link management is making sure that every section and page smoothly links to other relevant pages. Make sure those links from inside the body of one article pointing to another part of the site are consistent. That is different from the navigation of the whole site.
- *Version control.* This is related to work flow. You have to make sure that every piece of content on the site has gone through a reader approval process. You need to make sure that everyone is

working on the same version. Many times multiple versions of the site's content are floating around and a lot of energy is wasted correcting and commenting on dated material.

- *Work flow.* A process of getting an article through many draft versions; you want to get the latest version on the site. You don't want to have to go back through the site and start tearing it apart because content wasn't approved and edited in advance.

  Every different kind of article may need a different type of approval process. For example, a legal article or articles that have legal and liability implications may need to go through the legal department. Organizations may need actual verification for other news. Managing that with the changing of hundreds of articles a day can be a complicated process.

- *Localization.* This is the process of making your site content available to international users, which may mean translating your navigation or your content or both. Trying to keep all of those versions coordinated can be very difficult.

What are technical issues you are concerned about in a large e-commerce site?

The main ones are:

- *Transaction integrity.* This means that if a customer's credit card gets charged, he actually gets the product. The truth is that most e-commerce sites are pulling together a lot of information. They are pulling together payment processing and catalogue management and will frequently tie into inventory management and warehouse operations.

- *Security.* This covers a lot of territory ranging from protecting people's credit card numbers to not allowing consumers to make changes to the company's site. They have to secure their purchase patterns, which are a huge source of value. Purchase patterns, site usage, and demographics must all be protected and are very valuable to the company. You also don't want people to be able to place orders without paying for the goods.

- *Scalability.* This is a much bigger problem than people realize. Too often during the requirements phase, people think of the growth of the Web as being linear, and the truth is that it is exponential. The rate at which site traffic can grow is frequently a surprise to people. They underestimate what it takes to process the transactions. Most modern sites are crafted for N-tier solutions, which makes them inherently more scaleable. It is usually a mistake that people think their sales volume will go from 1,000 to 10,000 in a year—it actually happens in a month. With the rapid growth of the number of Internet users, plan on the number of visitors to your site being larger than you projected or coming sooner than you projected. Naturally, if you aren't publicizing the site, this won't be an issue, but if you are heavily marketing the site, you don't want the site going down or users not being able to access information.

Do you have different concerns if you know the site is either business-to-consumer (B2C) or business-to-business (B2B)? If so, what are they?

Yes, they are slightly different. They tend to fall into three different categories.

- *Target platforms.* B2B tends to have a narrower range than B2C in terms of browsers that need to be supported. Because of business security concerns, a public B2B site will have to avoid technology like Java and Active X. Corporate users will generally have access to newer but not necessarily state-of-the-art browsers. In B2B, you won't really have old stuff on corporate browsers. In B2C, the consumer can be using anything and it may not be the newest and latest versions so you have to plan for that.

Finally, you have extranets and intranets where you have very tight control over the browsers and the technical capabilities. A certain level of technology is a requirement for a certain level of access to the site.

- *Granular security.* On a B2C site, basically customers have access to the entire site. Although there may be parts of the site that you can gain access to only by providing certain demographic information or paying a fee, there isn't much differentiation between users. On a B2B site, though, it is more likely that individual users will have specific profiles and access to different parts of the site.

  A company like E*Trade is a B2C but acts like a B2B in that you want users to have access only to specific parts of the site that they have paid for by being a client of the company.

- *Billing mechanism.* In the case of the consumer, the vast majority of transactions use credit cards. In the case of a corporate consumer, you use real and virtual credit cards. They have other, much more complicated, purchasing mechanisms like purchase orders and EDI.

Is it better to buy off-the-shelf products than custom-developed applications?

The problem is the same for every business. They have very nicely packaged tools available. Rarely do you have to customize such technology as credit card validation.

It is almost always the case that the user interfaces and overall graphic design and site navigation is going to be custom developed.

Do most off-the-shelf products require some type of customization?

Yes! More and more are designed with customization in mind. That customization can range from very sophisticated administration tools to calculators.

What type of long-term planning do you advise your clients to do?

In terms of long-range technology planning, it is almost a requirement that every plan is a short-term plan. You need to rethink your strategy every twelve to eighteen months, and that may mean rebuilding your site and system. The question is, when will webtv, cable modems, and DSL (digital subscriber loop) be common and affordable to everyone? Once they are, you will see much greater use of video and more interactivity. It's hard to predict when to design sites to take advantage of those capabilities.

If I want to build a site along the lines of Amazon.com, I-Village, or National Football League, what type of financial commitment, short- and long-term, should I be thinking about?

In terms of long term, you will spend whatever amount you spent to launch, upgrade, maintain, and improve the site over twelve months. If you create a good site, someone will match and exceed your site, so you have to spend money to stay ahead of the competition.

To build sites like Amazon.com and I-Village will always cost you over seven figures. A couple of factors that play into the cost are sophistication of the design and the complexity of the infrastructure required to support it. If you are doing a news site that is changing every day, then you have to look at the costs of people, tools, and workflow. Finally, you need to develop a written plan that details how the site will be updated, who will be responsible, and outlines a budget for the site.

If your objective is to inform people about products and services that are going to be delivered through traditional channels, then you may be spending very little. If you are integrating real time into a manufacturing and fulfillment system, you can spend a lot of resources on that.

What skill sets do my internal people interfacing with outside developers need?

No one has an infinite budget. Web sites, even the best ones, are a morass of compromises. The people involved in developing and maintaining the sites have to have a good understanding of what the Web is capable of, but they have to compromise. The role of the outside developer is to help them get the most value for their budget.

They also need to be very active communicators. A good consultant will make a point of proactively telling clients what they need to do.

The reverse is also true. A good client will make sure the consultant understands what it takes to make really good decisions. Another skill that is useful is product design. Typically, product managers are good at integrating marketing and technology requirements and balancing conflicting requirements between them to get a system built.

Frequently, the sponsors of e-business initiatives will be senior marketing or IT management, but most Web initiatives have to be a happy marriage between both of these. The client needs to look at both sides of marketing and technical and understand the need, but it usually isn't their job.

Is it better to manage one's own site internally regarding changes and upgrades in technology, or is it better to outsource?

It depends on the focus of the company. The technology changes quickly. Unless you are willing to make a big financial commitment in terms of buying technology and training your people, then you are better off outsourcing technology changes. Given the business model of most Internet service business, it makes more financial sense for the company to manage content itself.

What causes a site to fail technologically (insufficient hosting capabilities, etc.)?

Technical failures can be attributed to a poor quality assurance (QA) process that forces you to discover bugs at your customers' expense well after site launch. People confuse quality assurance with quality control. The difference is that QA starts during the design and requirements process and ensures the quality of the design, architecture, and construction.

The worst case is a poor QA process that relies on final test to flush out architectural and design problems, because it is inevitable that the final test period gets squeezed by schedule slippages.

Another cause of failure is not planning for enough capacity. If you have done your job well and crafted a successful site launch marketing campaign, you need to be prepared for it to be successful. That may mean acquiring temporary capacity for site launch while you figure out what the site traffic will be. A site that performs poorly or not at all will never get a return visit.

Finally, you have to provide for continuous competent technical support for the site. Even if you don't make any changes at all, computers go down for no apparent reason. Redundant systems and fail-safe systems are complex and expensive and they are not a good substitute for strong technical support for both your servers and Internet connections.

Chapter Summary

The importance of preplanning your Web site and taking the time to screen the right developer can't be stressed enough. Smart planning involves the following.

1. Listing content requirements.
2. Listing interactivity requirements.
3. Listing who will be responsible for providing content internally.
4. Listing what parts of the site will be connected with other parts of the site.
5. Listing the priorities in order for the developers.

Finally, don't make constant changes during the development process. This will frustrate everyone involved. Once the site is up, then re-evaluate the site and make changes.

Chapter 3
Developing a Marketing Plan

VENTURE CAPITALISTS, MONEY MANAGERS, and stock analysts have one major concern that overrides all other concerns when it comes to investing in a company: "How does your company make itself heard over the noise?"

Any company can buy all of the technology it needs to put its Web site on par technologically with the best of the best. How easy your Web site is to navigate, the quantity and variety of products you offer, and how well your shopping cart works are important, but what matters most is that your target audience knows you exist.

What follows is an interesting chart that shows you how competitive the market place is, culled from doing a search in Yahoo! on the business words listed.

Word	No. of Categories	No. of Sites
Books	80	17,239
Computers	154	21,615
Health care	101	12,525
Investing	6	472
Music	120	27,061

Word	No. of Categories	No. of Sites
Toys	40	3,569
Travel	80	16,514

It's likely that you are surprised at the number of categories, let alone the number of Web sites in those categories. I am sure you have greater appreciation for the category leaders such as:

- Books: Amazon.com
- Computers: Dell
- Health Care: Dr. Koop
- Investing: E*Trade
- Music: CDNow
- Travel: Priceline

Four Keys to a Good Marketing Plan

1. **Understanding your audience.** Talk to your potential customers and find out what publications, broadcast shows, and Web sites they read, listen to, and visit. All too often companies guess or put their trust in their advertising firm. Go out and speak to your customers. I had a client that was buying lottery winner payment streams. It thought winners would go to a Web site that listed all of the states that sold lottery tickets and where one could purchase tickets for those states. When I spoke to my client's prospects and customers, none of them said they would go to such a Web site because they already were winners and didn't buy lottery tickets anymore.

2. **Media selection.** Get media packages from every type of media outlet you are considering, and put together a spreadsheet that has the following information:

   - Reader/viewer demographics
   - Number of readers/viewers
   - Issues with biggest readers

- Show topics with best draws
- Cost for running ads
- Cost for sponsoring promotions

Augment and cross-check your own media plan by having an outside firm put together a plan for you. I firmly believe outsourcing media buying is the best way to go because media buyers, through experience and contacts, know who can deliver what is written in their promotional material. Also, media buyers can extract discounts because of the volume of deals they are doing.

3. **Advisory board.** Put together a user advisory board and run your marketing strategy through them. I have found that advisory boards, which are entrenched in a particular industry, know what has and hasn't worked from speaking to their colleagues. As an example, one of my clients was marketing his product to trade associations. One of our board members had a lot of experience with trade associations and said the approval process was so long and the support from the association was usually so shallow that it would be a waste of time. My client redirected his sales force to focus on two other groups that ultimately turned out to be keeper distribution channels.

4. **Survey.** Speaking with your customers is great, but you probably can't speak to as many in a short enough period of time as you can through a survey. Make your surveys no more than ten questions and ask the users to fax or e-mail back the responses.

Marketing Tactics

To make money and be profitable, you don't have to be the category leader, but you do have to be able to grab the attention of users and drive them to your Web site. Like in football, all of the good teams have to execute the basics of blocking and tackling. To drive traffic to your Web site, you have to develop a marketing plan that utilizes some of the following ten weapons:

1. Affiliates
2. Banner advertising
3. Broadcast media advertising
4. Direct mail
5. Direct e-mail
6. Event sponsorship
7. Free content
8. Partnerships
9. Print advertising
10. Trade shows

Not all ten weapons are useful or should be used by all companies. For example, if you sell B2B and your niche is selling products or services to individuals who run pension funds, you probably wouldn't want to buy broadcast media advertising. The cost to reach your target market would be exorbitantly high for the return. Naturally, if you were selling business insurance, the rewards of utilizing broadcast media should far outweigh the costs since there is such a large pool of buyers who need your insurance. Chances are that your message would reach these buyers.

You will notice that I didn't mention public relations in the list of essential weapons. Public relations is a must for any online venture. Unfortunately there are very few unique concepts, which makes it difficult to get the media's attention. To be a long-term player, you have to be a savvy marketer and that means knowing how and when to use the ten weapons I have listed.

Example: Savvy marketers don't have to spend a lot of money to build their brand. One of my clients is focused on the professional artist industry. It is building brand awareness and attracting customers by cosponsoring events with student and professional artist regional trade associations. It bought a targeted e-mail list that was checked twice a year, and had a stipulation put in the contract that if 20 percent of the e-mails were incorrect or didn't exist, a discount of 20 percent would be taken off of the bill.

Before you look at the sample marketing plan at the end of this chapter, see the following description of each weapon and how it can be used to drive traffic to your Web site.

Affiliates

Affiliates are other companies that are willing to promote and sell your product or service on their site. The affiliates provide a link from their Web site to your Web site.

Advantages: Affiliates provide more visibility, they know their market better that the sponsoring site, and they are the lowest cost of sales acquisition. I, along with over 500,000 other Web site owners, am an affiliate of Amazon.com.

Disadvantages: According to International Data Corporation, only 2 percent of affiliates are driving sales to the sponsor site.

Cost: The only cost to the sponsor is the initial setup and mailing of checks periodically (monthly or quarterly) to affiliates. Once you are an affiliate, there is no cost to the sponsor because everything is automated.

Key to success: Affiliate programs fall prey to the old 80/20 rule—80 percent of your sales will come from 20 percent of your affiliates. Therefore, you need to get as many affiliates signed up as possible. If you are a B2B company, make a list of the Web sites you would most like to affiliate with and go after them. If you are a B2C site, grab all of the real estate you can and don't look back.

Banner advertising

Banner ads are like display ads in print publications. What makes them unique is that they can use animation, video, and sound to grab your attention, and once you click on the advertisement, you are sent either to a larger message or the Web site of the advertiser.

Advantage: Anyone who clicks on the banner is likely to be a real prospect or the person wouldn't waste his or her time going to the ad. It is a great way to separate yourself from your competition when someone is looking up your field or category on a search engine.

Disadvantage: A lot of times no one clicks on the banners and no traffic is driven to your site or the separate site setup to educate the potential buyer. If your banner is placed with a lot of other banners, potential buyers can get confused and move on to another page.

Cost: One of the costs is the development of the banner, which is usually a few thousand dollars. The real cost obviously is where you decide to run the ad. Ad prices are based on impressions (the number of times someone clicks on a particular page or advertisement), and impressions are based on the number of users who go to a particular section of a Web site. A site like Yahoo! can cost $10,000 or more a month. Some lesser traffic sites can cost more because of their user base.

Key to success: Give people a reason to click on your banner. That means offering large discounts, giving away prizes, and offering something that the prospect will find only if he clicks on your banner. CBSMarketwatch, the popular business news Web site, could offer free subscriptions to the first ten people each day that predict the close of the stock market correctly. This would be a good way to attract attention and capture names of potential users.

Broadcast media advertising

Broadcast media encompass television and radio. B2C sites that need to reach the masses typically use these media. For companies like CDNow and eBay, for whom practically everyone is a potential customer, building brand awareness is what separates those who survive from those who don't.

Advantages: It's a great way to reach a lot of people and become a household word.

Disadvantages: If not everyone is eligible to buy your product, such as books, CDs, or toys, then you are spending a lot of money to educate people who couldn't care less about your product or services.

Cost: Creating a quality commercial will cost in the hundreds of thousands. According to the Direct Marketing Association, the amount of money it takes to build a brand name using broadcast media costs in the millions.

Key to success: Develop a jingle or commercial that everyone will remember, and make sure the domain name is repeated every few seconds. You want domain name on the brain. Amazon.com's radio ads in 1999 equating the size of their online offering to filling the Rose Bowl were brilliant. They provided the listener with an image of a large stadium filled with books.

Direct mail

Internet companies send letters with a screen shot of their home page, postcards with the home page on the front, and brochures with the home page on the front and screen shots and written descriptions of what can be found on the site.

Advantages: It is still the best form of non-Internet based one-to-one advertising. You get to select the appropriate target audience by demographic and geographic. The chances of attracting users through this method of marketing are much greater than display or broadcast.

Disadvantages: People are so inundated by mail with pictures of Web sites that they are becoming less curious with each mailing.

Cost: The cost for a direct mail piece ranges from $.20 per mailing for a four-color postcard, stamp, and label to $10 to $15 to send a more elaborate type of brochure piece.

Key to success: As with banner advertising, you need to give people a reason to open your mailing and go to your site. A good way to get people to come to your site is to offer your product/service for free or something of value. The mailing should have a prize number that the prospect has to type into the site. By doing that you have captured the name of someone who actually came to the site.

Direct e-mail

Direct e-mail works similar to direct mail except the promotion is all done online. Unlike mailing-list houses that provide you with labels of the names you pick, e-mail houses like Bigfoot.com allow you to pick the demographic you are looking for and then they distribute the e-mail for you. If you were a beer company and wanted to reach men between the ages of twenty-five and thirty-five, Bigfoot.com would contact someone like ESPN or Sports Illustrated to leverage their e-mail lists, if they were available.

Advantages: Most people still open up all of their e-mail, according to International Dataquest, and people who receive e-mail have usually asked for the information that you are providing.

Disadvantages: You don't get a list of names, addresses, and telephone numbers to follow up with.

Cost: The cost ranges from $1 to $3 per name and $.01 to $.03 per e-mail.

Key to success: You absolutely have to offer something of value for free to get people to go to your site and fill out some basic information. You need to build your internal database so you aren't a prisoner of the e-mail houses.

Event sponsorship

There are many types of events you can sponsor, ranging from trade shows to seminars to awards dinners.

Advantages: You are getting in front of the audience you believe would have an interest in your product or service. For example, online investment banks like WitSoundView are ideal sponsors for venture capital conferences. The companies that attend venture capital conferences are the next wave of initial public offering candidates. As a sponsor, you usually get your name in all promotional material related to the event, which builds up name awareness.

Disadvantage: If you are sharing a sponsorship and you can't get one of your people to be a master of ceremonies or someone with visibility at the event, few people will remember your company.

Cost: Event sponsorship typically runs from ten thousand to hundreds of thousands of dollars.

Key to success: You want to be the only one or one of two from your particular field as a sponsor. You don't want to be one of five e-commerce companies selling computers at a health care show.

Providing free content to other sites

A lot of destination sites are in need of content to fill their pages. Free content is the most valuable content because they don't want to have to hire or buy content, which increases the expense of running their site. Home furnishing sites welcome the written thoughts of expert builders who can provide free advice to their users.

Advantages: You are recognized as an expert, and at the end of your column is your company's Web site address, which should produce new traffic.

Disadvantage: There are no notable disadvantages because you aren't paying for the placement of content.

Key to Success: You want to be associated with sites that focus on your market space. If you provide marketing advice to pharmaceutical companies, it doesn't do you any good to have your information found on the Staples Web site.

Partnerships

Partnerships are a good way to cross-sell your products. Bank of America and Citigroup have developed destination sites for business people to buy products and services. The two banks get a commission for each transaction, and with large transactions, they get the opportunity to fund the transaction itself.

Advantage: If your partner has a good name brand and/or a strong following, like Citigroup, the partnership will give you credibility and visibility.

Disadvantage: You must be astute in how you pick your partners. Unlike affiliates, the partner you've chosen can significantly impact how you are perceived in the marketplace. A client of mine that bought structured settlements, which are payments made from one party to another over a period of time, usually years, decided to affiliate with a site that promoted lotteries. Users of the site thought my client provided credit to gamblers and it attracted the wrong type of traffic.

Costs: The price of partnership can range from exchanging mailing lists and putting each other's banners on your sites to providing commission free revenue.

Key to success: Pick your partners wisely. Make sure they are as committed to success as you are and that their Web site is run like an entrepreneurial company and not some forgotten division. It is important that the leader of the Web site you deal with has autonomy and doesn't have to get the approval of five vice presidents and the board of directors.

Print advertising

According to Advertising Age, the print media have seen a tremendous surge in display advertising spending due to the need for Web sites to bring in traffic.

Advantages: You can pick the industry and the geographic and demographic markets. Readers tend to rip out and keep advertisements that are of interest to them.

Disadvantage: Ads are often lost in the fray. One ad tends to blend in with another.

Cost: Depending on the circulation, you could spend $5,000, for a quarter-page or half-page advertisement in a regional or niche publication, to $50,000, for a full-page advertisement in a national magazine like Vogue.

Key to success: Your advertisement has to be sharply written and placed where your target market would read it. Running one time is a waste of money. You need to budget running three to six advertisements in the same publication. The ad shouldn't be so cute and clever that no one knows what you are talking about or who you are.

Trade shows

Trade shows bring together people who are actually interested in a particular industry or product line.

Advantages: The traffic that comes to a trade show is either buyers or influencers with a smattering of tire kickers. Trade shows like Internet World provide a tremendous source of leads.

Disadvantages: Trade shows don't give companies exclusivity in terms of shutting out the competition.

Cost: The cost usually runs from $1,000 for a regional trade show to $100,000, depending on your booth size.

Key to success: It's not the size of your booth that determines success—it is the location, the way the products/services are presented, and a memorable giveaway. Companies that give away T-shirts are viewed as high-end substantive, whereas companies that give away candy give the appearance that they are hanging on by their fingernails.

Sample Marketing Plan
Marketing Plan for Krasner Interactive Philadelphia Metro

Executive Summary: This is an overview of the plan that we can share with the DC office, corporate, and new employees. Some of what is written is well known, but new employees will find it will help give them some focus.

Krasner Interactive is a 600-person, fifty-office public company that supplies Internet, Intranet, and Extranet solutions to Fortune 1000 companies.

According to Krasner Interactive corporate, "Krasner Interactive's Internet expertise enables Krasner Interactive consultants to provide strategies and implement business solutions that help impact profitability by increasing revenue, controlling costs, or enhancing productivity."

The Philadelphia Metro office is focused on obtaining business from Philadelphia to Harrisburg to Delaware to Central and Southern New Jersey. The goal of the Philadelphia office is to have $10 million in sales within five years.

Purpose of Plan: The purpose of this plan is to outline a sales/marketing course that will allow Krasner Interactive DC/Philadelphia Metro to increase its shareholder value under the existing buyout agreement.

History: Krasner Interactive Philadelphia is a new office with no history. It is part of the Washington, DC, office.

Krasner Interactive's Current Customer Base: Krasner Interactive's customers range in size from $1 million to billions in sales. They don't come from one particular industry.

Krasner Interactive's Strengths and Achievements Include:

- First strictly Web site development company to go public
- Over 1,000 Web sites developed on a national basis
- Only Web site company to have a national presence with over fifty offices nationwide
- First Web site company to have an international presence

Present

The Philadelphia office has had only one client, a law firm called Fox Rothschild. Krasner Interactive Philadelphia has no specific area of expertise at present.

Goals

Short Term: Krasner Interactive Philadelphia Metro's goal is to bring in $1 million worth of new business in 1998.

Long Term: Krasner Interactive Philadelphia Metro's goal is to bring in $20 million in revenue by 2003.

Mission

This section allows us to state what we believe our mission is.

The mission of Krasner Interactive Philadelphia is to be the leading developer of sophisticated Web sites in the tri-state. This means developing Web sites that require large backend databases and electronic commerce solutions.

Competitive Advantage

- National/International presence: Krasner Interactive has offices in fifty cities.
- Size and resources: Over 300 technologists.
- Experience: Over 1,000 Web sites developed.
- Partnerships with top technology companies: Intel, Microsoft, Pamdesic
- Leveraging knowledge across network. No other Internet company has this size advantage, which is very important as technology changes so rapidly.

Objectives

Short Term: 1998–2000
Financial:

- Develop $1 million worth of new business in 1998
- Develop $2 million worth of new business and develop $1 million from existing customers in 1999
- Develop $4 million worth of new business and develop $2 million from existing customers in 2000

Visibility:
- Run six seminars that attract 180 new prospects
- Appear six times in regional newspapers
- Write a monthly column for one to two regional publications

Personnel:
- Hire two consultants/salespeople, one or two full-time project managers, and one full- or part-time proposal writer in 1998 focused on pharmaceuticals and manufacturing
- Hire two consultants/salespeople to focus on insurance and banking

Long Term: 2001–2003
Financial:
- Develop $6 million worth of new business and develop $3 million from existing customers in 2001
- Develop $9 million worth of new business and develop $4.5 million from existing customers in 2002
- Develop $13.5 million worth of new business and develop $6.75 million from existing customers in 2003

Visibility:
- Run ten seminars per year that attract 300 new prospects
- Appear twenty-six times in regional newspapers
- Write a monthly column for four to five regional newspapers

Personnel:
Hire two consultants/salespeople, one or two full-time project managers, and one full- or part-time proposal writer in 2001–2003 focused on medical instruments and service firms.

Marketing Overview

This section provides information on how we will market the company to prospects and current customers.

Marketing Package:

- Brochure on services
- Flowchart on our process
- White paper
- List of URLs by industry
- Client endorsement letters

Note: The package doesn't have to be crammed with material. We want people to actually read what we send and find it valuable.

Presentation Materials: (PowerPoint presentation)

Replicate selected collateral material in PowerPoint (laptop) and on foils include info specific to the prospect. Eventually we want to develop a CD-ROM that has changeable modules.

Joint Venture/Lead Partners:
Accounting:

- Arthur Andersen
- Asher & Company
- BDO Seidman
- Bowman & Company

Direct Marketing:

- Devon Marketing
  - McClure Group
- Worldwide Marketing

Sponsorships/Memberships:

- Chemical Manufacturers Association
- Chester County Chamber of Commerce
- Delaware Valley Manufacturers Resource Center
Mass Mailing to Target Audiences:
- Postcards with Web site on them
- Letters to prospects that include only a white paper

Trade Shows:
- Select targeted industries
  (For less targeted or general: Drop off old brochures)

Events to attend: (Attended by top executives)
- Bauer Awards at Franklin Institute
- Borrower's Ball (Philadelphia Free Library)

Initial Letter: Here is a sample letter.

Dear Mr. Smith:

I recently joined Krasner Interactive as a partner in the Philadelphia office. We would like to invite you to participate in a panel discussion on how you use the Internet for customer service, marketing, and internal communications. The attendees will be high-level executives who oversee their company's Internet strategy and deployment.

A little background on Krasner Interactive—we have over fifty offices nationally and internationally. More than half of our employees are technologists, who graduated from the finest schools and have worked with top-tier companies. Fully 25 percent of our employees are business consultants with vertical expertise, who advise clients on marketing and implementation issues. We have built over 1,000 Web sites and are developing 500 Web sites at one time.

Enclosed in this package you will find a list of URLs we have developed for your industry, white papers that you will find of interest, and a description of our services.

I will call your office within the next week to discuss your participation in our seminar series.

Sincerely,

Marc Kramer

Partner

Success Seminar Series: This was touched on already, but developing a quality seminar series will raise our visibility and put us in a position to bring in and retain business.

Newsletter: We need to develop a bimonthly or monthly newsletter that is in both electronic and paper form. The newsletter, which would augment the white papers, would have the following:

- Tips on marketing a Web site
- Tips on best use of graphics
- Tips on how to build a quality Web site without spending your entire budget
- Information on new technology and how that would be used to bring in new business or retain existing business (problem with most articles on new technology is that there are few examples of how it has been used and the impact on the bottom line)
- Web master of the month
- Surveys

(We could use a tabloid type newspaper format and sell advertising to our vendors like Microsoft, Intel, Reuters, etc.)

Profile of Target Market(s): This section provides a profile of our target industries and the names of specific companies in each industry.
Overall Profile:
- 200 employees or greater
- $50,000 or greater Web site development budget
- Electronic commerce or ability to extract information from databases critical
- Important client service tool
- Ability to sell products online

Primary Target Industries:

Chemical and Petrochemical—Specialty lubricants, solvents, catalysts and reagents, plastic, and other resins

Needs and Interest:
- Employment information
- Inventory control
- Product information
- Safety information

Target Companies:
1. Arco
2. Betz Dearborn
3. DuPont
4. Henkels

Traditional Insurance—Insurance companies that sell health and commercial insurance.

Needs and Interest:
- Access to claims information
- Access to price quotes for field agents
- Access to accounts for independent agents
- To inform clients about new services (I know an insurance broker that is now selling prepaid legal insurance.)
- To inform clients about new offerings from existing carriers
- To inform clients about changes existing carriers are making
- To inform clients about different types of insurance they should consider as they grow and evolve

Target Companies:
1. Aegean
2. Aetna/U.S. Healthcare
3. AIG

4. Cigna
5. Chubb Group of Insurance Companies
6. Corporate Dynamics
7. Engle-Hambright & Davies

Biotechnology/Pharmaceuticals—Companies that develop and sell consumer drugs.

Needs and Interest:
- Educate doctors
- Educate sales force
- Find new drugs
- Provide FDA with information
- Provide safety and education on company drugs
- Train employees
- Communicate with investors

Target Companies:
1. Astra Merck
2. Cephalon
3. Centocor
4. McNeil Pharmaceuticals
5. Merck DuPont

Brokerage Houses—Send to director of marketing.
Needs and Interest:
- Account access
- Online trading
- Ability to view analyst reports
- Ability to select brokers
- Map and addresses of brokerage offices

Target Companies:

1. Alex Brown
2. Brown Brothers Harriman
3. Dean Witter
4. Legg Mason

Commercial Banks—Send to vice president of marketing.
Needs and Interest:

- Online banking
- Investor relations information
- Loan rates and applications
- List of branches
- New products
- Press releases

Target Banks:

1. Bank of Boyertown
2. Commerce Bank
3. Downingtown National Bank
4. First Financial Savings Bank

Electronics Companies—Send to president and vice president of marketing.
Needs and Interest:

- Pictures and information about parts
- Information on new products
- Support information
- List of distributors
- Employment opportunities along with employee applications
- Investor relations information

Target Companies:

1. AMP
2. Ametek
3. CFM
4. Fisher & Porter

Competition: This section focuses on Krasner Interactive's primary competitors and what their strengths and weaknesses are. This helps Krasner Interactive better position itself with prospects and helps employees focus on what makes Krasner Interactive unique.

Primary Competitor	Strengths	Weaknesses
Cambridge Technology Partners	International Cash rich Stock rich Good reputation Great client list	Expensive
Integrated Consulting Group	National Big pharmaceutical base Cash rich	Poor Web dev.
US Interactive	Regional Good client list Strong graphics capability	Too general

Secondary Competitor	Strengths	Weaknesses
Actium	300 technical people Strong client list	Not known for Web dev.
CoreTech	200 technical people Strong client list Extensive database dev. Exp.	Not known for Web dev.
Group Cortex	Good client list 15 technical people	No money
Magic Fox	Good client list	No money
TM Group	Good client list Strong e-commerce cap.	Avg. mkting

Chapter Summary

After you have finished your business and Web site plans, you need to develop a strategy to attract and retain users. There are four steps to developing a good marketing plan.

1. **Speak to end users.** Have a third party interview your potential users and ask them what they think of your site and how it compares to competitor sites. It's better to have a third party ask the questions because it has no stake in the site and cares only about providing the owner of the site with an unbiased opinion.

2. **Obtain a competitive analysis.** Have a third party perform a strengths-and-weaknesses analysis of your competitors, and ask what it will take to surpass the competition.

3. **Build an arsenal of marketing weapons.** Develop a list of ways you plan to market the site, create a budget, and ask end users what forms of marketing would grab their attention.

4. **Develop a realistic budget.** Make sure your budget will support your plans. Marketing is about consistency and getting into and staying in the prospective users' minds.

Chapter 4
Selecting the Right Consultants

THREE YEARS AGO there was a handful of companies that knew how to develop complex content and e-commerce Web sites. Now there are thousands of companies around the country that can develop just about any type of Web site you want. The key to picking a good developer is to look at five to ten Web sites that most resemble what you are looking for, and then interview their firms.

There are six essential issues you should discuss with each developer you interview:

1. Scoping fees
2. Project manager
3. Experience and team location
4. Technology
5. Price
6. Quality assurance process

Scoping Fees

All of the large Web site developers require a company to pay for the developer's people to spend time with those in charge of developing the

Web site to get an understanding of what the company is trying to accomplish from sales, service, and marketing perspectives. This is crucial because it impacts the look and feel of the Web site and how it interacts and connects with other parts of the client's business.

Value of Scoping Fees Example

I had an international client that was providing its clients with access to twelve different databases that it used to provide on CD-ROM. The developer needed to know if the clients were individuals who reviewed information from their home computers or were working on a computer at a company that had a fast connection.

The developer needed to know what type of databases the information was housed in and how users would get to the information and in what form they would view the information. Finally, the developer needed to know how many people might simultaneously want access to the databases, and if this company would be using video and audio in the future to provide information.

Project Manager

You want to get an experienced project manager. The amount of money and the complexity of the project will determine who is on your project. In the case of large development companies like Razorfish and US Interactive, your project must be a minimum of $250,000 or you end up with the second team. Don't scrimp when developing a complex site. A good project manager will save you time, money, and reduce the aggravation factor.

Interview the project manager and ask the following questions.

1. What is the most complex site you have overseen development of?
2. What made the site complex?
3. What problems did you encounter and how did you resolve them?
4. Have you ever been over budget on a project and what did you learn from it?
5. What is your methodology for developing my site?
6. How many people are on your team?
7. How often should we meet in person?
8. What is your turnaround time for meeting milestones?
9. When we want to make changes, what is your process?
10. What is the best way for us to work effectively so you meet my needs?

Picking the Right Project Manager Example

A large international information provider was providing access to all of its databases through the Internet. The company interviewed a variety of developers and selected one of the larger companies in the industry. The company asked many of the right questions, including if one of the people representing the developer at the meeting would be the project manager. One of the developer's senior managers said he would be overseeing the project, but didn't say he would actually be managing the project. The company felt comfortable with the developer's senior manager and signed the contract.

Unfortunately for the company, the senior manager wasn't actually managing the project and had delegated it to a junior person who reported to him. He, in fact, was running five sizable projects at one time. The company had never asked or thought to interview the junior person and ask what experience

he or she had at developing large multilanguage, mul-
tidatabase accessible sites.

The final result was that the company paid
$500,000, and the chairman fired most of the internal
people involved with the project and instituted a whole
new team. The chairman of the company learned
enough from the experience that he asked each
prospective developer of the new site to send only the
person who would actually be managing the project to
meet with him and two of his other managers who
would be involved with the Web site. He then pro-
ceeded to grill each project manager about the experi-
ence and time commitment he or she would bring to
his project. If the Web site wasn't done properly, com-
petitors could overtake their position as the top
provider of information for their industry, and there-
fore the selection of the project manager was critical.

Experience and Team Location

The Internet was supposed to allow companies that develop Web sites
to service people thousands of miles away. Unfortunately most buyers
like to know that they can hop in a car or catch a train or plane and
meet their developers face to face without going across time zones. In
the beginning of any project, there is a lot of face time. Either hire a
consultant who has vetted a lot of developers or use a service like
rfpMarket.com that sends your proposal to developers and matches
your needs by profession and geographic criteria. Once you view the
sites of the firms you would like to consider, go and make onsite visits
to see if they actually have the horsepower to deliver what you need.

Picking an Experienced Developer Example

One of the companies featured in this book is a sizable e-commerce company. It went through an extensive selection process to pick the right developer. The three major criteria were cost, experience, and physical location. The company developing the site was a small regional developer that had built some semilarge complex e-commerce sites. It didn't charge up-front consulting fees, and it promised the client that cost for the first phase, which would have things up and running by Thanksgiving (approximately six to eight weeks away), would be less than $80,000.

The developer had the technical know-how but didn't have a proven process for developing large complex sites that require access to multiple databases. The developer also didn't have enough depth of developer talent to get the project done in a timely manner. The site launched after Thanksgiving and had a strong reception, but users found that they couldn't buy what they wanted because an error message kept coming up. A week after Christmas, the site still wasn't working properly. The CEO of the company said he should have made experience the top priority and paid whatever he needed to pay to have the right company develop the site.

Technology

Every buyer asks every developer if it uses off-the-shelf solutions, which theoretically will cut the cost and time of development. Large complex sites with many product offerings can use off-the-shelf products, but in most cases they require some degree of customization. What a buyer wants to know is that the developer has technologies it has developed for other clients that can be plugged in or that require only minimal customization.

The Importance of Technology Development Experience

Large Web development companies such as Razorfish, Cambridge Technology Partners, and Lante have developed so many complex Web sites that they have a variety of tools and software that can fit just about any need. One of my clients, ECRI.org, who is featured in this book, developed a destination site for hospital administrators. He chose Aspeon to develop his site because it had experience with complex sites and lots of usable technology. The site cost in the high six figures to develop, but it was done correctly.

Price

Allowing a developer to build a site on time and materials is a scary proposition. Always select a fixed price contract and have the contract broken down so you can see what each part costs. You will inevitably find sections that you can do yourself or reduce the amount of time and price the developer is going to charge for that section. For example, the developer might have a charge for registering you with all the various search engines, which is something you can and should do yourself. (Domain registration companies such as *www.register.com* charge $35 to register your Web site with the 300-plus search engines found on the Internet. Registering with various search engines increases your chances of attracting visitors to your Web site.) Another example is providing the actual copy and putting it into HTML. Not difficult with today's tools. If you want to learn about the newest software to develop Web sites, go to *www.Webtools.com*, and if you want definitions about different concepts or products related to the Internet, go to *www.Webopedia.com*.

Opting to go fixed price will keep you and the developer focused on the overall budget, and if you have to adjust the budget, then you will make that decision. I tell my clients to put aside 20 percent of the fixed price contract for overruns. Most times the overruns, which are usually changes in the graphics or text of the Web site, are not the fault of the developer but of the client wanting to make changes that weren't agreed to when the contract was signed.

Example of Controlling Costs

A large international travel company was building a Web site for consumers to use to book their vacations. The company hired an experienced developer, but the executives who were managing the project on the client side were inexperienced. The developer was asked to provide its hourly rate and a fixed price proposal. The developer told the client that it could build the site for $350,000. Believing the developer padded the numbers to protect itself and to walk away with a sizable profit, the client insisted on paying on a time-and-materials basis.

The client spent $75,000 on a site map because the client was disorganized in its approach to collecting information from the various departments involved in the project. By the time the project was completed, at a cost of two times the fixed price contract the developer originally offered, the senior managers involved with

59

the project were met by security at the front door of the company, handed a box with their possessions, and told to find employment elsewhere.

Quality Assurance Process

Every developer claims it has a quality assurance process. Ask your prospective developers to provide a written process of how they make sure the site is functioning properly before it goes live. The quality assurance people are as important as the development team. They need to be meticulous. The process should work as follows:

Step One: The project team reviews each section. It doesn't review the sections it works on because it probably won't see its own errors. After the team has reviewed a section, that section should be sent to the internal person responsible for quality control.

Step Two: Quality control develops a spreadsheet with the name of each section and subsection. They then review each section and sub-section and provide a list of changes to be made.

All grammar and sentence structure is reviewed thoroughly. Nothing infuriates a client more than getting materials to review that are laced with spelling and grammatical errors. I will never forget the time one of my largest clients left me a voice mail one night asking me "how could I ask them to review materials that weren't even thoroughly reviewed by our people." And the person went on to say that if they had given their CEO the site to look at, that people could have been fired.

Step Three: There should be four to six people reviewing the site—two or three from the client's side and two or three from the developer's side. They should each get a spreadsheet similar to the one the quality control person used for the first review. Each day a specific section should be reviewed, and the quality control person should make one list of changes and hand it over to the project manager. The project manager should inform the quality control person when the changes have been completed, and the quality control person should check each item off of the list.

Step Four: The quality control person should ask the client to initial each section once it has read and approved all of the changes.

Quality Control Performed Well Example

A large international consulting firm was developing a sizable content destination site to demonstrate its knowledge and depth to clients and prospects. Being a consulting firm, it knew that it had to appoint one person as supreme commander over the project so there wouldn't be too many people interacting with the developer.

The consulting firm's project manager brought in two firms to develop the Web site: one firm to develop the front-end graphics and content and the other firm to handle user access to various databases. The manager in charge from the client side requested that a formal quality assurance document be prepared for internal and external people to review the site before it went live, in order to catch all of the mistakes. The review sheet was simple and easy to use and required the reviewers only to type in the mistakes they noticed by section and page and e-mail them back to the consulting firm's manager in charge of the project.

A very smart move made by the client, because the external people found enough errors that the launch date of the site was pushed back by almost a month to ensure the site would be mistake free. They believed that if their clients reviewed a site that was riddled with errors, confidence in their ability to deliver quality would be eroded and competitors would use the site's mistakes as a way to win business.

Chapter Summary

Smart planning is essential to developing a successful Web site business model. Next to hiring the right management team, which we will talk about in the next chapter, it is essential to evaluate and hire the right people to develop your site. When selecting developers remember the six elements for successful Web developer selection:

1. **Scoping fees.** Try to do as much of the planning as you can to minimize the amount of time your developers need to spend in creating a technology plan for you. Accept the fact that you will have to pay some amount of money for the developer to understand all of the technical needs of your business in order to build a quality, enduring site.

2. **Project manager.** When evaluating project managers, think of them as if they were going to join your organization full time. If you wouldn't hire them to work in your organization, then don't retain them to work on your Web site. Make sure they understand and have had the experience of developing a site similar to yours.

3. **Experience and team location.** The reason we hire people to do anything is because they have had both successful and unsuccessful experiences at doing what we need them to do. Make sure the organization and the team within that organization have suitable experience.

4. **Technology.** Try to use off-the-shelf products or technology created by your developer that has been tried, tested, and shown to work. Avoid at all costs having to develop technology from scratch. It is both costly and unpredictable.

5. **Price.** Don't fixate on price. Obtain three quotes from three developers who have successfully developed the type of site you are building and then worry about price. Stay away from time and material contracts because the developer and your own internal staff forget that the company doesn't have an endless supply of money to throw at your site.

6. **Quality assurance process.** Take your time and do it right. The old saying related to first impressions being important fits perfectly when describing what a company needs to present to the world. All good developers have a written quality assurance process and online forms for their clients to use. Don't walk—run—away from any developer that doesn't have a process to ensure that the end product will be error free or close to error free.

Chapter 5
Web Site Hosting

DEVELOPING A GRAPHICALLY ENHANCED, feature-rich, easy-to-use, database-laden Web site is great, but if the hardware and Web site hosting solutions you choose don't match what you invested to develop the Web site, you will have wasted your money.

Companies with little or no experience at developing and managing Web sites that have an abundance of content and product offerings coupled with the potential for a large number of users often underestimate the site's technology requirements. I have had clients read an article in a newspaper or read the advertisements in industry publications such as Interactive Week and see that they can have their Web site hosted for as little as $10 a month. My clients aren't so unsophisticated as to believe they can have their sites hosted for such a small amount of money, but they are usually left numb when they see the true costs of hosting the type of site they have built or want to build.

There is a big difference between managing and hosting *www.kramercommunications.com*, which basically is made up of thirty-plus pages of HTML (hyper text markup language), and a large international consulting firm with hundreds of pages or an e-commerce site with hundreds of products and thousands of customers visiting the site each day. You need to make thoughtful technology decisions. The last mistake you want is for your site to crash when clients and prospects come to visit.

There are two issues that companies need to consider when deciding how to manage and host their site.

1. In-house control (buying and servicing a dedicated computer within the company to host the Web site)
2. Outsourcing

You will notice that I didn't mention budget. The market will dictate what you need to budget regardless if you decide to manage the technology internally or outsource it.

Outsourcing

My recommendation to clients is to outsource and focus on your business. Buying, installing, maintaining, and staffing to manage one's own site is very costly and a huge headache. There are three steps to making the right outsource selection:

Step One: Develop a Request for Proposal

In order for a Web hosting company to respond to your proposal, it needs answers to the following ten questions:

1. How many megabytes of space will your site take up?
2. How many daily, weekly, and monthly users do you anticipate?
3. What type of security do you require?
4. Will you want to own the hardware/server the Web site is hosted on?
5. Will the company be responsible for making sure the server is restarted if it goes down?

6. Does the company want to just rent space on one of our servers and have the hosting firm manage it 24/7?
7. What language is your site written in?
8. What type, size, and number of databases will need to be hosted?
9. Who is responsible for upgrading the software for the databases?
10. Does the company require its site to be on its own server or will it share a server with another company?

If you are developing an e-commerce site, the following additional questions will be asked by a hosting service:

- Does the company want to offer online payment options with credit cards or e-checks?
- Does the company want to have secure transactions via Secure Sockets Layer (SSL)? (SSL works by encrypting data that's transferred over the SSL connection.)
- Does the company require online order tracking features?
- Does the company want orders relayed to a fulfillment house?
- Does the company want to review and retrieve orders via a Web interface?

I have a client who is particular about what types of companies the hosting company has as clients. It does not want to be hosted by any company that would host pornographic material.

Below is a sample price list from a regional hosting company in Pennsylvania, called Bee.Net. This will give you an in-depth understanding of all the issues a hosting company deals with and the variety of packages offered by hosting services.

Web Site Hosting Packages

prepayment period:	Value	Standard (Most Popular Package)
	perfect for brochure type Web sites	includes Web site statistics, FrontPage, ASP, & ODBC
monthly	$40.00	$50.00
quarterly	$105.00	$135.00
Best Value! yearly	$400.00	$500.00
One Time Set-Up Fee	$50.00	$75.00

In addition to our excellent support services and hosting on our high availability network, the following features are included in the package pricing:

Web Site Hosting and Maintenance

registration or transfer of domain name: www.companyname.com	yes	yes
Internet fee for registration of domain name, (not applicable to transfers). Includes use of domain name on the Internet for one year.	$35.00	$35.00
Windows NT 4.0/IIS 4.0 server hosting	yes	yes
password protected, unlimited 24/7 FTP access for editing site, using any Internet access account	yes	yes
Web site storage space	20MB	50MB
monthly bandwidth allowance	2GB	5GB
toll-free phone and e-mail technical support	yes	yes

E-mail features

number of separate e-mail accounts	4	4
additional e-mail boxes (no setup fee for additional boxes added at startup)	$10 setup fee, plus $5/month, $15/quarter or $50/year	$10 setup fee, plus $5/month, $15/quarter or $50/year
unlimited incoming e-mail aliases via wildcard alias *@domainname.com	yes	yes
mail forwarding option	yes	yes
access to e-mail from non-Bee.Net Internet access account via any Internet mail software	yes	yes
Web browser access to e-mail	yes	yes
Web browser based e-mail account administration	yes	yes
e-mail auto responder feature	yes	yes

Web Site Marketing Features

homepage counter cgi	yes	yes
listing in Bee.Net Gallery	yes	yes
Webtrends Web site statistics www.domainname.com/stats/	- -	updated monthly

Web Site Developer Product Support
(upon request)

form to e-mail processing using Formalis WebFormLite for single forms or Formalis WebForm for multiple forms	yes	yes
Microsoft FrontPage 2000 server extensions	- -	yes

69

Web Site Developer Product Support, *continued*
(upon request)

Allaire Cold Fusion 4.x support	-	yes
ASP (Microsoft Active Server Pages) support	-	yes
Microsoft Visual InterDev 6 support	-	yes
MDAC 2.x and ODBC database connector support (including MS Access 97 and 2000)	-	yes
CDONT / SMTP support	-	yes
PHP Hypertext Preprocessor support	-	yes

Optional Web Site Services

additional storage space	$10/10MB/month
additional bandwidth	$10/100MB/month
Verisign SSL encryption for form processing—using Bee.Net's certificate	$25 setup fee, plus $20/month, $55/quarter or $200/year
Verisign SSL encryption for form processing—using your own certificate.	$50 setup fee, plus $55/quarter or $200/year $349 initial and $249 annual fees paid to Verisign $20/month,
ActiveState Perl support	$25 setup fee, plus $20/month, $55/quarter
Microsoft Visual Basic 6 cgi support	$25 setup fee, plus $20/month, $55/quarter or $200/year
Microsoft SQL Server 7.X support (includes 30MB database space)	$50 setup fee, plus $25/month, $70/quarter or $250/year
additional domain name pointing to same content	$50 setup fee, plus $5/month, $15/quarter or $50/year

Optional Web Site Services, *continued*

Hypermedia ECware shopping cart (fees include SSL, setup of Web server environment, and license to use software on Bee.Net's server)	$500 setup fee, plus $40/month, $110/quarter, or $400/year.

Add Dial-Up Internet Access

modem or v.90 Internet access— interactive use only, pricing per user This discounted pricing is available if the related services are included in the same billing and payment as the Web site (see *http://local.bee.net* for Bee.Net's listing of access phone numbers)	$20 setup fee, plus $15/month, $45/quarter, or $180/year
ISDN Internet access - interactive use only, pricing per user, (does not include Verizon fees)	$20 setup fee, plus $34.95/month, $95/quarter or $350/year

A proposal for hosting services to evaluate doesn't have to be long, but it has to answer the aforementioned ten questions. The following is a sample request for proposal (RFP) I sent out on behalf of one of my clients.

Sample Request for Proposal

Request for Proposal

Contact: Marc Kramer, Kramer Communications

Client: Entertainment Company

Background: The client is a major motion picture company. Their current site receives two million hits a month. Because they are a major motion picture company, the following are important when hosting the company's Web site.

- Ability for users to have access to up to 200 distinct Web sites, each having its own domain name.
- Ability for users to download QuickTime and RealNetworks video and audio streaming technology. These video/audio clips can range from 30 seconds to 15 minutes.
- Ability to buy products related to the movies developed by the company online. The reason for mentioning this is to make sure the server is compatible with various e-commerce technologies ranging from shopping carts to credit card transactions to store credit card data to securely taking the transaction online.
- Ability to handle a million users simultaneously. This would occur twice a year: the Oscars and Grammys.
- Ability for company Web master to know how often each page is being hit on each site owned by the company. This would include daily, weekly, and monthly numbers. The client would like to be able to access those numbers in real time from its PC.
- Hosting service must have the capability to move current site from its current service to the new hosting company's servers.
- Hosting service is responsible for keeping site up and running 24/7.

Additional Vendor Requirements

Speed	T-3
Other hosted sites	No pornography
Sharing of server	Company needs to have its own server
Server technology	State of the art, upgraded annually
Backup system	Company needs to have site mirrored
Transfer cost	Cost to transfer site from one host to new host
Time to transfer	How fast can transfer be done and site up
Ability to change content	Procedure for changing content
No. of mailboxes supplied	Although supplied by parent company, would like a price on mailboxes
Ability to check traffic	Need to check daily site and page usage
Security	Must be Secure Key Card or comparable technology

Current Setup

Site Categories	Current
No. of servers	2
No. of gigs	Machine 1 = 4 disks: 2 x 2.1 GB int/ 2.1 GB Ext / 9.1 GB Ext
	Machine 2 = 4 disks: 4.2 GB int/ 2.1 GB int/ 4.2 GB ext/ 4.2 GB ext
Current hardware platform	Machine 1 = Sun Ultra 170 / 256 memory
	Machine 1 = Sun Ultra 1200 / 320 memory
No. of domains	8 on 1 machine. None on the second.
Video streaming	Uses QuickTime for short pieces

Current Setup, *continued*

Site Categories	Current
Audio streaming	Uses QuickTime for short pieces
E-commerce	Yahoo! store
No. of visitors	An average of 2+ million hits per day
Special times	Oscars and the Grammy awards—2 million users
Database	Oracle—all databases developed in Oracle
Average monthly data transfer	An average of 325 GB +
No. of Jpegs	Number of .mov files: 423
	Number of .avi files: 421
	Number of .jpg files: 3,179
	Number of .gif files: 1,300
	Total bytes: 2.6 gigabytes
No. of mailboxes	Supplied by corporation
Security	Servers require either a Secure Key Card or S/Key technology

Step Two: Evaluating Proposals

It can't be emphasized enough that if you are developing a large Web site, you have to spend as much time evaluating your hosting company as you do evaluating the developers who built it. There are five questions you need to ask when evaluating hosting proposals:

1. Do they understand what we are trying to accomplish?
2. Do any of their clients have similar hosting needs?
3. How many certified database developers in the technology my site uses do they have?
4. How many full-time people do they have monitoring their servers?

5. Do they have a second facility that mirrors their primary facility in case of fire or some other hazard that causes their systems to go down?

During the course of the last year, I have had the opportunity to review a lot of hosting proposals. The companies I have found to be best at understanding complicated sites were the ones who had well-thought-out proposals and asked questions related to the number of users, Web site functionality, security needs, and scalability of the Web site. In the example of the media company, we had small hosting companies telling us they could host the example for a few thousand dollars a month. On the other end, we were getting proposals from large hosting organizations that said it would cost $15,000 to $25,000 a month.

One of my associates who served as an acting CIO for a variety of companies reviewed the proposals for my client. He ended up recommending Digex based on its proposal and discussions with it. My associate has reviewed numerous proposals, but he thought Digex had a better understanding and solution than any of the others we were evaluating.

Step Three: On-site Visit and Customer References

Don't solely take a hosting company's word that it can deliver the solution you need. Make sure you visit its facilities and speak to its customers. One of my clients was changing hosting services and had three companies make presentations to him. After reviewing the presentations, he selected a company. Before signing the contract, I suggested we make an unannounced visit.

When we visited the company, we found that it was in an old manufacturing building in an economic redevelopment zone. That was no problem for me or the client, what were problems were the condition of the facility and how lax the security was. There was no receptionist, and we were able to walk around undetected for a good five minutes.

75

Finally, someone saw us walking around and asked if we needed help. We asked for a tour of the hosting facilities. During the tour, we noticed that there was no alarm system. We asked why there was no security and were told that few visitors ever came to the facility and that the front door and windows were heavily secured.

After the visit, we decided the risk of using the company was too high. We visited the next company on the list and found that its offices and security were first rate, but its clients weren't happy with the overall service they were receiving.

In-house Management

There are companies who prefer to operate their own hardware because of the proprietary nature of their business or just because they don't like to cede control to an outside company. The types of companies who usually prefer to manage their own operations in-house are companies that deal with highly sensitive issues or are concerned about user privacy because of the nature of their business. Companies in the financial and medical fields tend to want to protect their most valuable assets and give users a sense of security.

The following is a question-and-answer interview with Russ Wetherell, chief technology officer at Bee.Net, who talks about the differences of hosting Web sites internally as opposed to outsourcing hosting, and about how to figure out an appropriate budget for hosting.

When does it make sense to host your own Web site?

If you already have the bandwidth, network infrastructure, and qualified staff.

When you need to maintain control over the operating system configuration as well as hardware. You need to integrate your Web server with other data stores that currently exist within your company and are dynamically updated all the time.

What are the pros and cons of having your own server?

Pro: Complete control over the operation, environment, and security.

Con: Need staff or consultants readily available to set up, configure, and troubleshoot problems. Bandwidth costs are high.

When does it make sense to colocate your Web site, and what are the responsibilities of the owner of the site and of the hosting service?

When you need to have control over the server hardware and software configuration. When you need a higher level of data security and integrity. Typically the hosting service is responsible for supplying a secure location with adequate power and 24/7 monitoring systems, bandwidth, routing, and DNS services. The site owner would supply the hardware, OS, and Web server software as well as proof of insurance.

Do most hosting services have a second copy of their client's site in another server located in another location?

I can speak only for Bee.Net. We do not mirror content, but we do have regular backups to tape. Our contingency in an emergency is to colocate servers with our broadband providers and restore from tape backups.

There are some larger hosting companies that do mirror Web site content at other locations for redundancy and disaster planning.

How do you figure out your hosting budget for an e-commerce site?

It really depends on the level of technology and sophistication that the site owner/developer requires. We have four core pricing structures and then add additional features a la carte. E-commerce sites tend to be resource intensive on both the server and bandwidth. The OS environment has to be carefully configured and maintained by qualified staff. This is particularly important in a shared server/hosting environment where a misbehaving program running on one site can start to affect the performance and operation of other Web sites on the same server.

How do you figure out your hosting budget for a content-oriented site?

We base our budgeting on hard drive storage space and bandwidth. All Web sites are allowed a set amount of drive space and bandwidth. Excesses are billed on a per unit basis over and above the subscribed amount.

Chapter Summary

When evaluating what type of hosting solution your site requires, remember to consider the following:

1. **Size of the site.** The size of the site dictates the amount of space you will need to purchase, which affects the cost of hosting the site whether you are outsourcing hosting or buying your own hardware.
2. **Number of users.** Knowing the number of projected users is important because you will want to know if the hosting companies you are considering have the hardware and telecommunications capability of managing large amounts of traffic.
3. **Internal control.** If your site changes hourly or daily or you have a lot of sensitive information on the site, you may want to own your own servers.
4. **Outsourcing.** When evaluating hosting services, make sure they have the experience and resources to host your type of site.
5. **Hardware costs**. Make sure that the hardware you purchase, whether it is colocated with an outside hosting service or on your premises, is scalable. You don't want to move your Web site from one hard drive to another, because it is time intensive.

6. **Software costs.** Make sure the hosting service has the appropriate software to support your site. If you are managing your own site, you will need to consider the cost of licensing and supporting new software.

7. **Personnel costs.** If you manage your own servers, you need to consider the cost of hiring a server administrator. Many times the cost of hiring an administrator is much greater than the cost of outsourcing hosting.

8. **Number of e-mail boxes.** This will depend on the size of your site and the number of individuals who need e-mail addresses.

9. **Security.** Make sure, whether you host your own Web site or outsource hosting, that you have the proper physical security and most recent security software so no one can tamper with your site.

Chapter 6
Strategies and Implementation for Long-Term Success

LONG-TERM SUCCESS IN MY GRANDFATHER'S DAY was a business that was passed down three or four generations like the House of Rothschild in Europe. In my father's day, long-term success was having a business that was successful for at least a quarter of a century and being traded publicly on the New York Stock Exchange. Today, long-term success is measured in five- to ten-year increments.

If anyone had told my grandfather and even my father that the local electric company in Philadelphia, which had been around for as long as there has been electricity, would be owned and operated by a company in Chicago, they would have thought it was a joke. Long-term success in the Internet is not much different than building a successful venture prior to the creation and acceptance of the Internet. It's all about smart planning and execution.

When I work with a company, there are three levels of success we focus on regardless of whether we're building a site from scratch or upgrading an existing Web site. I want to make sure the owner of the site is creating new sales opportunities, retaining clients, and reducing client service costs. We review the company's business and marketing plans and site and corporate marketing materials. After the review, my staff and I make written recommendations on how to improve sales, reduce costs, and retain current users.

Level One: Web Site Strategic Objectives Checklist

1. **User.** The number of users the company hopes to attract for each of the first five years. Why is this important? Because this will determine the type and hard drive size your site will require and the level of customer support that will be needed. If you are expecting a million users a month, then you are looking at a pretty hefty Web site hosting bill. Chances are you are going to have the site's contents distributed over a few different servers. If you were selling products, then you would want more than two or three people answering questions. Nothing frustrates a buyer more than poor customer service.

2. **Revenue.** If the company is selling their product or is providing a service that is delivered by the Web, then we need to know what the financial objectives are and tie them in to how the site should be developed. For example, if the company is selling to other companies and it sells only ten products but each product is $100,000, then we are probably talking about a Web site that is rich in pictures and other types of graphics. The users obviously want to see what they are buying. We know that a graphic intensive site won't be a problem because a purchaser of this type of product probably has a very fast connection and download time isn't an issue.

   I have a client called tendollars.com, which is selling 10,000 different inexpensive gifts. The site is a B2C site. It is using thumbnail pictures that the user can click on and increase in size. By making the pictures small, the download time will be reduced and the user won't get frustrated and move to another site.

3. **Client Service.** Many companies such as Dell Computers and Intel use the Internet to reduce client service costs. They list all of

their products and replacement parts on their Web site and allow the customer to choose and click what they want.

There is a new technology that has been developed by a company in New York called M-Pen. The technology uses an animated talking character that walks a user through whatever problem he is trying to tackle.

4. **Visibility Building.** The objective may not be making money or reducing costs, but rather enhancing visibility and building brand awareness. There are companies such as ESPN, the all-sports cable television distributed show, that want to increase their brand awareness and not lose viewers. Anyone can buy sports information and game videos from college and professional teams, so the barrier to entry isn't very high. The only barrier is name recognition.

Level Two: Technical Functionality

If you go to Internet World, the preeminent trade show for anyone doing anything with the Internet, you will see hundreds of technology companies spread out over the equivalent of four to five football fields. These companies are selling the latest internal and external search engines, customer service applications, audio and video streaming technology, and Web site developer tools for using Java and other programming languages, to name a few of their wares.

When you are constructing, rebuilding, or improving your Web site, you need to keep five elements in mind for developing and implementing a technology plan:

1. **Customer needs.** You need to understand what kind of information the customers want, how they want to receive it, and what type of machine they typically use. If you are J. Crew, the relatively expensive clothing company, then you know you are selling to consumers using home computers. Dell Computer has the positive

burden of serving both B2C and B2B markets, so they have to develop for both types of customer needs.

2. **Internal technology management.** If the information systems department is responsible for upgrading the site, then the CIO needs to take inventory of his staff and technology licensing agreements. The CIO has to know not only his internal Web site developers' and programmers' capabilities, but he must be equally aware of their limitations.

3. **Internal integration.** Companies that use Microsoft NT as their server platform want to make sure their Web sites, especially if have they have databases connected to them, aren't developed for another platform such as Unix (Webopedia.com provides the following description of Unix:

> UNIX was one of the first operating systems to be written in a high-level programming language, namely C. This meant that it could be installed on virtually any computer for which a C compiler existed. This natural portability combined with its low price made it a popular choice among universities. Due to its portability, flexibility, and power, UNIX has become the leading operating system for workstations. Historically, it has been less popular in the personal computer market, but the emergence of a new version called Linux is revitalizing UNIX across all platforms.

> The information systems (IS) department doesn't want to have to serve two technology masters.

4. **External integration.** Many times companies who have e-commerce sites don't do their own order fulfillment or customer service (or both). Yet, the company's internal system has to be able to integrate with external systems it connects to in order to facilitate a seamless flow of information.

5. **Educating outside IS.** The IS department becomes frustrated when people outside the department want to make technical decisions without including it, because when those decisions end up failing, it is expected to clean up the mess. It is important that IS review, consult, and approve all technical decisions related to the Internet. At the end of the day, the CEO will look at IS if anything goes wrong.

   Here is the list of technical needs IS must be aware of:

- Customer applications
- Database search and retrieval capability
- Download time
- Ease of electronic commerce options—catalogue and cash register
- Ease of use and accuracy of site calculators
- Ease of navigation
- E-mail
- Graphics
- Links to other sites
- Screen view on 15- and 17-inch monitors
- Use of audio
- Use of video
- Use of programming languages such as Java
- Use of leading-edge technology
- Proper technology planning

Web Site Content Checklist

The marketing and communications departments need to make sure that the site has the appropriate customer service information so clients and prospects don't become frustrated when trying to find important information. As respected as the Dell Web site is to order computers and accessories from, it is maddeningly difficult to find corporate contact information. Before your site goes live, make sure you have the following on your site:

- Company telephone number
- Company e-mail address
- Company mailing address
- Educational information
- Executive contacts
- Individual customer service contacts
- Press releases
- Testimonials
- Site map

Customer Feedback

Every day I remind my daughter, Ariel, that she is the CEO of her own company called Ariel. I tell her that her customer is her teacher and instead of paying her in money, the teacher lets her know if she is getting what she ordered by giving Ariel a grade for each product she hands in. I encourage her to constantly ask the teacher to clarify what she wants when she is unsure.

Throughout this book, you will find a common theme of getting to know and understand your customer. The difference between the great companies and those who are fighting to stay alive is customer service. Customer service is made up of the following:

- Product/service satisfaction
- Product/service improvement
- Face-to-face interaction between customers/prospects and management
- Face-to-face interaction between management and the vendors who support the company

What makes QVC, which is featured later on in this book, successful? Customer service! A large part of quality customer service is interviewing your customers to get their impressions of your company. What follows is an interview that exemplifies the importance of quality customer service and how to attain it with one of the leading interactive customer product and service companies.

Interview with Paul Mann

Paul Mann, cofounder and CEO of Informative, Inc., oversees overall operations, finances, and strategic initiatives for the company. Prior to founding Informative, Paul comanaged the successful startup of Team Alliance Technology Partners, a twenty-five-office nationwide IT recruitment and consulting firm recently acquired by Hall Kinion—a major multinational corporation. Prior to that, Mann held positions in business process reengineering, quality assurance, and sales for IBM, Estee Lauder, and the Inverness Corporation, respectively.

Informative, Inc., is the leading application service provider of Web-based, real-time information solutions. Informative's hosted applications collect and report mission-critical feedback directly from Internet users in real time, accelerating the ability for companies worldwide to understand the marketplace and make timely, informed business decisions.

What are the most common reasons e-commerce sites fail?

Do they have a good business model or not? Let's assume they do. I think primarily the problem was they weren't able to test the marketplace properly. There are so many points of failure. Companies now face a new market or paradigm.

The biggest disconnect we have seen is that companies aren't taking the time to do active, timely research on the market. Before you go out to the market, you should speak to the market.

Traditionally, companies have hired market research firms and have conducted traditional methods of market research, which can include telephone interviews, direct mail, and the like. That is dangerous on the Internet because the Internet is a visual medium and people can provide feedback only on things they have looked at and tried. In the Internet space, a powerful way to conduct market research online is to conduct concept testing for copy, packaging, and even banner ads by sending out e-mails to people to see their responses before the concept is live. We have developed a series of solutions to help e-commerce businesses discover why their customers aren't spending more money on their Web sites. Informative's targeted solutions can capture the valuable feedback of why customers visited their site and why they decided to leave. We report the feedback in real time to help our clients make quick adjustments.

Businesses can learn about site navigation, how effective one particular ad banner is over another, and why a good percentage of their online shoppers abandon the shopping cart process. It's about asking the market: Do we have the right products? Does the name help or hurt the company? What do you think of our competitor's site? Brand perception and positioning are very important.

To give an example, one of our clients had a spider in their logo and buyers didn't like it. It sent a negative message about the brand, affecting their revenues. A lot of owners/founders may like a certain logo, but they have failed to look outside of their bubble to determine what their buyers like. Owners/founders should always take into serious consideration the likes and dislikes of their buyers.

Why do buyers abandon their shopping carts?

Roughly 75 percent of online shoppers abandon their shopping carts, roughly 97 percent leave sites without ever making a purchase, and of those who do make a purchase, only 15 percent come back to purchase again.

There is not one reason but a whole host of reasons why this happens. Working with a major greeting card company, we discovered why customers left the site before making a purchase. They left for the following reasons:

1. I thought you were electronic greeting cards and you are paper based.
2. You are more expensive than going to a store.
3. I thought you were the WNBA basketball team.

Generally speaking, other, more obvious, complaints include slow load times, too many layers to click through, and insufficient inventory. There are thousands of reasons why your customers will leave your site before making a purchase, but you need to do the site-specific research in order to find out what they are.

What do merchants need to do to improve their chances of getting customers to buy?

Merchants simply need to ask customers what they want. Informative, Inc., helps companies through their entire life cycle. Initially, by providing concept testing to conduct site and brand testing; then providing demographic profiling and usability testing; then providing ad effectiveness and site satisfaction studies. These steps would be followed up by customer satisfaction surveys focused on the site's process, support, and product. Companies also need to find out if their ads have been effective and if the brand name creates positive or negative customer awareness.

Then you need to consider why you lost business in the first place. Why did they leave? Why did they exit their shopping cart? Why is there a lapse in repurchase from customers?

What types of information should a merchant ask for that will make future marketing to a customer easier?

Merchants should ask customers who they are, by conducting demographic profiling, and what they buy, by conducting product consumption/habit studies. The best thing to do is simply ask the consumer what they think. Customer feedback is an immeasurable source of information for the merchants.

How does a merchant get customers to give it valuable demographic and buyer information?

It's a combination of a few things. First, you need to ask intelligent questions.

Second, you need to create a compelling reason for the user to take the time to answer your questions. They need to feel like their answers and feedback count. Third, you should provide incentive for the customer to respond to your questions. They want to be rewarded for their time and effort. In the past, customers received a T-shirt or were entered into a contest. But I have a personal suggestion that I think is more exciting and motivating for the customer.

Informative has partnered with more than twenty leading charities worldwide to establish a unique Charitable Contribution Incentive Program that can be automatically included as part of a survey. The program allows survey respondents to select from a list of more than twenty well-known charities to donate a dollar amount that our client specifies. The money goes to the designated charity upon completion of the survey.

What's great about this is that it's not focused on "what I can get," but "what I can give." It's a win-win-win situation. The survey participant wins by helping the company and those in need, the company wins because respondents will take more ownership in the survey and will take the time to answer the questions thoughtfully and honestly, and the charity wins by receiving the donation.

Many companies put their CIO in charge of customer service. Should customer service have its own leader who reports to the CEO or president/COO?

That is a judgment call. Customer service is the most important thing you can provide to a client. I would be concerned if customer service didn't report directly to the CEO. I have a problem with customer service reporting to the technical department. I think they should sit at the same table with the other top managers speaking directly to the CEO. Of course, customer service does encounter technical problems that need to be addressed, but there are nontechnical problems such as marketing that also need to be addressed.

Should the CEO and/or customer service vice president provide their e-mail address so customers can speak directly to them?

I don't think it is a good use of the CEO's time to answer endless e-mails all day long. I think the CEO needs to set a tone so that people know how the CEO would answer. Hewlett Packard sets this tone well and wrote a compelling book called the HP Way, which sends the message about the importance of making customer service as great a priority as technology development or sales. I also like iPrint.com. For a small to medium-size company, they send a clear corporate message. They are consistent. They make a strong promise that they can provide fast, easy, and affordable printing through your computer, and they back it up with a guarantee. They walk the walk. It has a very consistent and effective tone.

Should the CEO and/or customer service vice president e-mail customers and ask if they can speak to them in person about their shopping experience?

CEOs do need to get out there and mix it up. They can't confine themselves to their offices and boardrooms and speak only with their managers. They need to talk with the customers so they can make

91

informed decisions. What is important is that everyone, along with the CEO, needs to stay in touch with the customer. One person can't be held responsible; everyone in management needs to talk to the company's customers.

I think that there are technologies like Personify that allow sites to make suggestions based on what others like the customers would buy. (Other technologies that improve the shopping experience are digital wallets that hold address and credit card information, such as *www.gator.com*, so a buyer doesn't have to keep re-filling in information every time he or she makes a purchase.) We still have a ways to go before we make it a real one-to-one experience between the company and the customer. We need to accumulate a lot of information. Things that shorten the search process are good for you. Creating lifetime discount programs and price clubs will help. At the end of the day, it really comes down to understanding who your customer is, what he wants, what you provide, and why this is beneficial to the customer.

Chapter Summary

Long-term success requires a company to focus on the following:

1. **Customer Technology.** You have to consider what type of computer, what speed modem, and what Internet access the end users have in order to determine the amount of graphics, animation, and video you offer on your site. Having a site that is overloaded with graphics and special features that take an excessive amount of time to download will frustrate the potential customers to the point that they go somewhere else and can cripple or even kill your business.

2. **Customer Service.** Keep in mind that picking the product is only part of the buying experience. A major part of the interaction between the customer and seller occurs after the purchase when the

customer needs assistance. If you rely strictly on posting answers to the most common consumer questions and there is no opportunity for human interaction, customers will not buy from you. It is essential to constantly interview your customers online and in person so that you can understand their present and future needs.

3. **External Integration.** If you are running an electronic commerce site that interacts with other systems outside of your own system, such as an order fulfillment system, make sure that your technologies are compatible. Also be certain that everything appears seamless to the user.

4. **Internal Integration.** Selecting the right accounting, customer service, and e-commerce applications and making sure that they all speak with each other is essential to running a smooth operation and improving efficiencies.

5. **Technology Usage.** Think through when is the best time and best use of new technology before deploying it. Many companies become enamored with new technologies only to find out that their internal systems can't support them properly and/or the customer finds them frustrating to use or of little to no value.

Chapter 7
Retail Gifts

EVERY DAY I READ VENTURE WIRE (*www.venturewire.com*), which provides press releases on what venture capitalists are investing in. I also attend five to six venture capital conferences a year along with the regional venture capital association meetings for Philadelphia and New York. According to what I read and hear, no one wants to invest in Internet retail concepts.

Internet companies such as Value America and Boo have gone bankrupt. The stock prices of Amazon.com and others have dropped by as much as 95 percent. The question people ask me is if the party for online retailers is over. I think the party has just started and a second wave of investment will emerge.

Five years ago, everyone bought his or her books at a bookstore. How many people do you know of who haven't bought at least one book online today? I personally have bought books, shirts, games, backpacks, and software over the Internet. I am even considering buying stamps over the Internet because I hate standing in lines at the post office.

I can't predict what will happen in the stock market, but all you have to do is look at the revenue numbers of companies like Amazon.com, and

CDNOW, which range from over $100 million to over $3 billion in sales to know this isn't a fad. The straight online retailers are only half the story. The bricks-and-mortar retailers have also set up shop on the Internet, including QVC, Wal-Mart, and Gap. Their online sales are growing faster than their traditional stores, and in many cases are actually augmenting sales in their bricks-and-mortar outlets.

Right now, American buyers are driving most of the sales for these stores, but as the world becomes wired, sales will be driven globally. Brand names like Amazon.com, QVC, Gap, and smaller companies such as Red Envelope will all benefit from increases in online international sales.

Six Reasons Online Retailing Will Succeed

The reason we are seeing a shakeout in online retailing isn't because consumers aren't buying; the problem for many of these companies is a lack of capital necessary to build visibility and create smooth technology infrastructures, and enough cash to allow sales to catch up with costs. Below are six reasons why online retailing will succeed.

1. **Ability to reduce and increase shopping time.** According to the U.S. Department of Labor, over 60 percent of American families have two wage earners. Therefore, personal and family time has become more valuable. The ability to buy what you need during a break at work or before the children get up or after they go to sleep has become a driving factor in the growth of B2C marketing.

2. **Ability to reduce prices.** Online-specific businesses like Amazon.com saw that by not having to make investments in building stores and having to build only warehouses, they could offer a discount on the price of every book they offered and that

they could offer every book in print. Shelf space is unlimited on the Internet.

3. **Ability to reduce the cost of doing business.** Amazon.com understood that buyers didn't need or necessarily want to go to a store to purchase music. The average bricks-and-mortar retail store, according to the Retail Merchants Association, typically averages $100,000 to $300,000 of revenue per employee. Egghead.com, which sells business and consumer software, closed its stores and now does over $1 million per employee.

4. **Ability to establish a one-on-one relationship with shoppers.** When a customer goes to Nordstrom's, the only way Nordstrom's knows what the customer is buying is if he uses a Nordstrom's credit card. If he uses the more popular MasterCard, Visa, or American Express credit card, Nordstrom's has no idea what Joe Smith and Sally Jones have purchased or what they might want to purchase in the future. However, customers who buy online provide a variety of information during a sales transaction, and the seller can capture that information.

5. **Ability to offer more products.** Three years ago, I went into my local chain bookstore and asked them if they had a copy of a particular book. The store carried over 100,000 books, but not the book I wanted. The manager looked at her computer and smiled at me and said they had the book in their warehouse and I could have it in two weeks. I mentioned that Amazon.com, which has access to 3 million books, could get me the same book in two days and she shrugged her shoulders.

6. **More people online.** One of the main reasons that retail sales on the Internet have grown from zero in 1995 to $20 billion in 2000 (according to Forester Research) is because 60 percent of Americans are now Internet enabled. Timely Internet access, thanks to faster modems, cable connections, and DSL, has made download times quicker.

A worldwide study of e-commerce by Taylor Nelson Sofres (TNS) Interactive found that among Internet users around the globe, 10 percent shop online during any given month. In addition, 15 percent of users say they have considered shopping online, but have not yet done so.

The research was based on more than 30,000 interviews in 27 countries on four continents. Not surprisingly, it found that the United States has the highest proportion of Internet users (58 percent of population) and also the highest proportion of shoppers (27 percent). In contrast, only 1 percent of users currently shop online in both Thailand and Turkey.

11 Elements to Developing a Successful Retail E-Commerce Site

Buying gifts and personal products online is still a novelty to those just getting Internet access, but for the millions of veteran cyber shoppers, a successful online retail business must do twelve things well.

1. **Web site functionality.** One of the major reasons people buy online is because they are looking for a fast, simple way to shop. Web sites that require users to click three or four times to get to a product and then a couple more clicks to buy a product turn shoppers off. In most cases, those shoppers never come back, and so every online store knows that the first impression is the most lasting and most meaningful. One of my clients experienced a variety of broken links on its site that caused it to lose tens of thousands of dollars each day. Now it is trying to lure customers back by giving them $25 gift certificates so they can see that the site problems have been fixed.

2. **Security.** The media has made consumers aware of the security risks associated with buying online by pointing to the one out of millions of transactions that results in someone hacking into a

Web site's database and stealing a customer's credit card numbers. With that said, buyers want to see that the Web site has implemented security encryption procedures to thwart individuals who look to use other people's credit to buy products.

3. **Product availability.** Nothing frustrates a buyer more than going to a Web site and, after spending considerable time in selecting a product, finding out that the company doesn't have the product and won't have it anytime soon. Buyers who went to the Toys R Us Web site in Christmas of 1999 were disappointed and frustrated to find out that the world's largest toy company didn't have many of the gifts that were advertised on its Web site.

4. **Product delivery.** Once the customer goes through the online check out and selects how quickly they want a gift to arrive at its intended destination, you better meet that expectation. Retailers must make sure that their online ordering system functions well with their shipping department. Many big name retailers such as Toy R Us were inundated with calls from irate customers who were waiting for weeks for their gifts.

5. **Customer service.** With the technology for the front end of Web sites improving so much that new and small companies can offer the same degree of interactivity and product selection as Amazon.com and Wal-Mart, the key to long-term success is quality customer service. Quality customer service will encourage customers to return to a company's site time and time again.

6. **Gift support.** Consumers, especially male consumers, need help in remembering important events in family and friends' lives. The companies who provide automatic e-mail reminders about when mom's birthday is coming two weeks before it happens will engender a thankful long-term customer.

7. **Human interaction.** Many times customers want assistance from a salesperson. The ability to connect from the Web site directly or call an 800 number and speak to someone in less than 60 seconds

is important. Companies that don't offer direct assistance or that make buyers wait for more than a few minutes risk losing sales, both short and long term. Unless the site buyers go to is the only one that offers a particular product, they will go somewhere else.

8. **Product tracking.** Once customers buy a product or service, they want to know who is shipping the product, what the tracking number is, and how they can follow the package until its safe and timely delivery.

9. **Easy return policies.** Customers expect the same easy return policies online that offline companies provide. Traditional retailers can swing the pendulum of customer interest back in their direction by letting dissatisfied customers return products bought online to their bricks-and-mortar locations. Online stores have to be able to provide customers with a telephone number to have unwanted gifts picked up at their door and sent back.

10. **Product support.** Companies that don't provide online and live product support or offer telephone numbers of the manufacturers' support units won't survive for the long term. Nothing is more frustrating than losing the box or support manual of a new product and not being able to track down the manufacturer to ask questions.

11. **Selection.** Successful online retailers have to offer either a large selection of gifts, products that are hard to find, or a depth of products for a particular area of interest such as fishing or antique car parts.

Examples of Success

Although the number of big name online retailers will likely shrink over the next year or so, the number of companies selling gifts over the Internet is growing exponentially because many regional companies and entrepreneurs are developing niche sites. I have interviewed two company executives who I think best understand how to build a quality retail Web site. I selected one pure Internet company and one non-Internet company that has made the transition smoothly.

Both companies have adhered to the eleven elements of how to build a successful retail e-commerce site. Below is a chart that will provide you with insights into the cost, building, and maintaining of a retail gift Web site.

	Red Envelope	QVC
Initial cost to build the Web site	$1–$5 million	$1 million
Cost to maintain Web site	$500,000–$1.5 million	$1 million plus
Full-time technologists/ content developers	10	35
No. of salespeople/ business development	1	3
Employee time commitment	50 hours per week	50–60 hours per week
Projected growth of sales department	2	None
Biggest day-to-day concern	Customer retention	Shipping and delivering
Marketing techniques	Banner ads Print advertising Direct marketing Outdoor advertising	Television
Best marketing techniques	Online portal placements	Television
Projected growth of marketing budget	300%	Very little
Strategic partnerships	None	Nickelodeon, Red Rocket
Retention techniques	Direct mail, e-mail	Event marketing

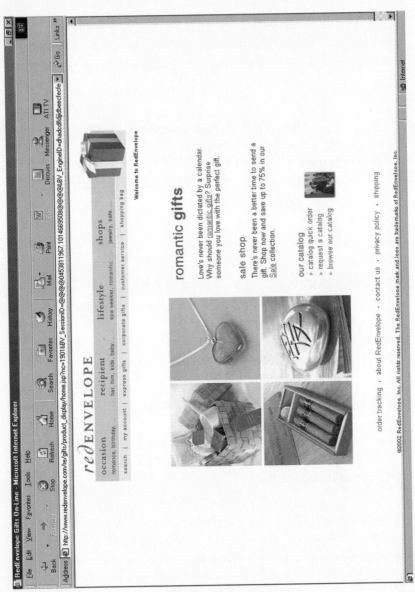

www.redenvelope.com

Red Envelope Interview

Hilary Billings brings over fourteen years of experience in the design and home furnishings industries to her position as President and CEO of Red Envelope Gifts Online. She was appointed to this post in July 1999 after having joined the company in May 1999 as Chief Merchandising Officer. Billings has been instrumental in the relaunching of Red Envelope, formally 911gifts.com. She has overseen all aspects of the redesign, including the name change, revamped site design, and the selection of a fresh, upscale product mix. She graduated from Brown University in 1985 with a BA in art history and English.

What are the three to five critical success factors by which you measure yourselves?

- Customer acquisition costs
- Repeat customer rate
- Customer lifetime value
- Product margin
- Gross sales growth

How important is first mover advantage?

It's important, mostly in terms of raising money; you want to be out ahead. It also helps in getting press and consumer mind-share. Building and improving the site takes time and experience; the earlier you get started, the better the experience will be.

What is the most difficult part of retaining users?

Finding the balance between maintaining a dialogue and over-communicating.

What types of skills are you looking for now? (Technical and nontechnical)

Technical skills: programmers, system administrators, database experts. Nontechnical skills: merchandising, customer service, and marketing, senior finance person.

What types of skills will you be looking for in the future? (Technical and nontechnical)

Technical: same as now. Nontechnical: corporate business sales-people.

What is unique about your site that makes users want to book-mark it?

A consistent, well-defined modern sense of style created by great merchandising vision, layered on top of a shopping experience that allows consumers to shop for gifts the way they want to.

What new technologies do you plan to deploy to make the user experience better that will result in more users?

We are looking at a variety of technologies such as streaming video and audio, but we need to see how quickly greater bandwidth for consumers becomes more readily accessible and affordable.

Traditional Internet Retailer Success Story

There are brick-and-mortar retailers who are trying to figure out how to capitalize on the Internet. They understand all of the advantages and they know the Internet is here to stay, but they are searching for a way to increase sales for the company overall and not just simply move money from one pot to another. QVC, which sells products on television and through company-owned stores, was an early adapter and, according to iQVC, was profitable from the outset.

iQVC

The addition of online service should increase the customer base and number of product orders while decreasing the cost of processing orders as the percentage of Web site orders increases. Additionally, the ability to increase the number of available products should increase the number of customers and advertisers.

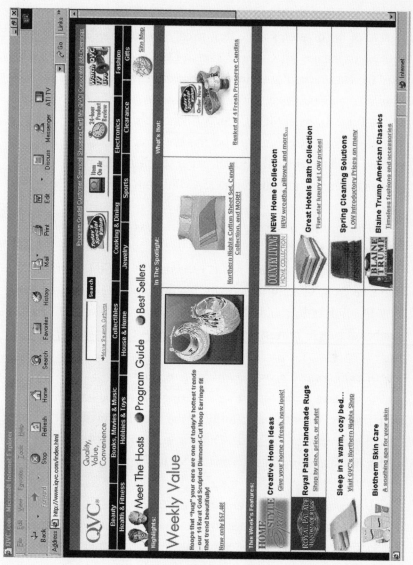

www.iqvc.com

iQVC Company Interview

Steve Hamlin is vice president of iQVC, QVC's online retail division. Steve joined iQVC in 1994 and has successfully overseen the development of the division's more than twenty-five-member staff and daily business operations since its inception in December 1995. He has supervised the construction of a virtual warehouse network of more than 300 individual suppliers/manufacturers that stores and ships products for iQVC. Prior to joining iQVC, Steve' honed his professional expertise over more than twenty years in product database development and relationship building within the manufacturer/supplier industry. He received a BA in business administration and an MEd from Kent State University.

What are the three to five critical success factors by which you measure yourselves?

(1) Obviously, number one is revenue; (2) profit; (3) the conversion rate from visiting to actually buying products (also known as look-to-book ratio); and (4) in our situation, we also evaluate the number of people converting from iQVC to QVC and vice versa.

What is your biggest day-to-day concern?

In the area of the virtual warehousing where you have third party ship. I worry about the immaturity of the suppliers in delivering merchandise directly to the home. Quick communication turnaround is a challenge. That is my biggest concern for iQVC.

How important is first mover advantage?

I think in the long run that it is not that important. For example, if you look at QVC—the Home Shopping Network started before us, but now we do more than twice their business. You need to do customer service, execution, and brand building well, and you will succeed. However, Amazon.com was a first mover and has kept ahead of the competition.

What is the most difficult part of retaining users?

To be successful you have to understand where the consumer is technology-wise. Our site is very highly skewed to women and that may have a bearing on retention strategy. We need to convert our QVC customers to iQVC, and that means we are giving them more than one way to buy our products.

What types of technical and nontechnical skills are you looking for now?

We are looking at different types of branding for our categories. We are looking for people who understand Internet commerce and applications. We want to build categories as separate brands. For instance, if you look at the cosmetic section of our site, we want customers to be able to select beauty aids and see how those products work for them.

What types of technical and nontechnical skills will you be looking for in the future?

We will be looking for people who understand how to build brands. As a company, we are always looking for technical skills and that will continue to be the case in the future.

What unique approaches are you using to retain employees?

We don't really do anything unique. We are large and growing with a good culture, and that provides stability and helps retain people.

What is unique about your site that makes users want to bookmark it?

What is unique is that we have a tremendous selection that covers many categories. What makes our site interesting is that we have unique brands like Joan Rivers and Victoria Principal. We have great brand names that the buyers trust. Harris Poll rated us number one for customer satisfaction on the Internet.

What didn't you expect that didn't turn out well?

We have done some technologies like a speed buy, which allows the customer to buy instantly. It hasn't gone over well at all, even though it's convenient. Customers like to go step by step. Maybe over time they will get comfortable with it.

Future Prediction

There are a lot of local differences, according to a report published by Nelson Taylor Sofres, a British research firm, that have emerged among the Internet-related shopping behavior in different countries. In India, for example, 83 percent of users have never shopped online and have no plans to do so, compared with 36 percent in the United States who don't shop online. The purchase of food and grocery products online is highest in Hong Kong (32 percent of users), leisure travel is highest in France (44 percent), and toiletries and cosmetics are highest in Japan (12 percent), compared to virtually none in the United Kingdom. Internet users in France buy the most stock and mutual funds online—17 percent, compared to 2 percent in the United Kingdom. Approximately 22 percent of online shoppers in the United States have purchased clothes online, compared to 10 percent in the United Kingdom.

In the United Kingdom, the same study found that 18 percent of the users had bought goods or services online during the past month. An additional 13 percent said they plan to shop online within the next six months. At the same time, just over 10 percent of the users said they considered buying online, but eventually decided against it.

Hamlin believes e-tailing is still in the "embryonic stage." "People are just starting to embrace the technology," Hamlin said. "With our kids it is going to be huge. The environment is going to change tremendously and fast. Comparing tomorrow will be like comparing today to 1900."

Billings believes that broadband, which will significantly increase the speed of how objects, pictures, and video download onto a computer, will have a huge impact on online retail because retailers will be able to show more than pictures of gifts to customers. Clothing sales will increase dramatically because users will be able to view themselves in the clothes they select and won't have to worry that what they purchase for themselves or a friend won't fit.

Chapter Summary

The key to building long-term relationships with customers is simple. If you do the following things well, you won't have to rely solely on spending enormous sums of money to promote your site.

1. **Easy Web site navigation.** Make sure your site takes into account that consumers, unlike corporate users, typically don't have high speed modems, so pictures and graphics should be programmed into the site in a way that download time doesn't cause the user to go to another site. Buyers should be able to find what they want and pay for it in less than five clicks of their mouse.

2. **Variety of choice.** Consumers expect more choices than a typical bricks-and-mortar store carries, because computers can provide an almost infinite amount of space to stock items.

3. **Depth of product.** Consumers hate to spend their time shopping and then entering the checkout line only to find the product isn't available. Make sure you don't underestimate the amount of products you need to carry. It is important to develop relationships with suppliers who can refill your warehouse shelves quickly.

4. **Easy return policy.** Don't make the customer beg and threaten for you to take back an unwanted product. The companies who have easy return policies build a strong bond of trust between the customer and the company.

5. **Strong customer service.** Don't assume that an extensive question-and-answer database will address your customer service problems. Don't make finding customer service people a treasure hunt. Nothing frustrates customers more than not being able to speak with a live human being about a problem, concern, or question.

6. **Know your customer.** The best way to develop repeat business is to provide your customers with information on products that they will want to buy for themselves or for others.

7. **Gift support.** The companies that send e-mail reminders of when important occasions like birthdays and anniversaries are coming up develop long-term relationships with their customers.

If you follow the above suggestions, your company will be the beneficiary of the strongest type of marketing support: word-of-mouth endorsements.

Chapter 8
Financial Services: B2C

ONE OF THE FIRST AND MOST SUCCESSFUL USES of the Internet has been the selling of financial products and information and conducting financial transactions. The amount of money that will be spent on financial services over the Internet, according to International Dataquest, one of the leading Internet research firms, will be over $100 billion over the next three years.

Companies such as E*Trade, an online brokerage company, have seen their sales go from $5 million to almost $300 million in the span of three years. Individual investors no longer have to wait to read the Wall Street Journal to learn what is happening to companies and industries they have invested in; they can simply find the information on the Internet.

Until the arrival of the Internet, consumers typically shopped for mortgages and home equity loans through their local newspaper, or they just contacted the bank they had their checking and savings accounts with. They bought their life, health, and personal insurance through local brokers or responded to direct mail from companies like Geico and Kemper.

Before the latter part of the 1990s, the only way to interact with your bank was to either go in person or, in some rare cases, make a telephone call. Eventually, only the largest banks with huge information systems departments were allowing customers to bank over the Internet. Today, even the smallest banks are allowing customers to do their banking online.

The Internet has dramatically changed the way consumers buy financial-oriented products and obtain financial information. The Internet has made for more knowledgeable buyers. The competition for those buyers is increasing exponentially every day. To illustrate the level of competition, we performed a search on Yahoo! using the major financial consumer needs as the match criteria. As you can see from the results in the following table, there are over 18,000 financially oriented Web sites.

Word	No. of Categories	No. of Sites
Banking	13	1,741
Financial news	6	821
Insurance	42	6,724
Loans	6	4,524
Stock brokerage	11	378

12 Elements to Building a Successful Consumer Financial Online Business

Today, there are so many semicustomizable solutions (products that can be adapted to anyone's business with some level of modification so they fit into and work with the buying company's technology) that practically anyone can get into the online financial services business. There is a site I recommend that will explain different types of Internet products and technology and assist you in finding vendors. I suggest visiting www.webopedia.com, which is part of internet.com.

Any bank, insurance company, insurance broker, financial planner, or brokerage firm that wants to develop a successful online business needs to incorporate the following twelve elements.

1. **Deep and timely research.** Consumers are looking for an edge. Therefore, the financial sites they use must have substantive and detailed information. Users go to sites like *www.sageonline.com* that provide detailed information and interviews with money managers, and sites like *www.cbsmarketwatch.com* and *www.fool.com* that provide information on stocks and bonds.

2. **Fresh content.** Early in the evolution of the Internet, users would go to a USA Today Web site and pick up the same information they could find in their newspaper. The only difference was that the information was changed with greater frequency. Sites like *www.ragingbull.com*, featured later in this chapter, provide timely information about public companies and what other investors think of those companies.

3. **Large product offering.** When consumers are shopping for new or additional auto, life, and home insurance, they want to solicit as many bids as they can for their business. The companies like *www.quotesmith.com*, which is featured in this book, and *www.etrade.com*, which allows users to buy stocks, bonds, and mutual funds, save the user time and money.

4. **Ability to compare products.** The companies that provide the greatest value allow the user to compare prices. If you go on Quotesmith.com's Web site, you can find out who provides the lowest rates and has the least amount of exclusions.

5. **Ability to retrieve purchase forms.** In the insurance business, a deal can't be consummated until the person signs an application. The sites that provide easy-to-download applications with a minimal amount of interaction with sales agents take away a part of the interaction that is uncomfortable for most buyers.

6. **Ability to buy products.** The Internet has significantly affected the stock brokerage industry. Intelliquest projects that by 2005, half of all stock purchases will be done directly by the buyer through the Internet.

7. **Ability to save money.** Insurance and stock brokerage firms are finding out that, for a sizable percentage of the buying market, the ability to do their own research and to purchase directly from the seller as ways to reduce costs are deciding factors in what, how often, and how much the buyer purchases.

8. **Ability to get human assistance.** Although buyers want the ability to save money and avoid salespeople, they still want the option of being able to speak to someone knowledgeable about the products they are purchasing. Companies who provide toll-free numbers and the ability to click on a button that has someone call them provide the best of offline and online customer service.

9. **Ability to monitor purchases.** Customers who visit *www.vanguard.com* and *www.fidelity.com* are able to see what stocks and mutual funds they have purchased. Both companies were early adopters of the Internet, to provide a higher level of customer service, reduce costs in mailing information, and increase purchases by making the process of purchasing products easier.

10. **Ability to cross-sell other products.** E*Trade started out as an online brokerage firm and now has moved into providing online banking services. Its next foray will be insurance, which will allow it to offer its customers a fully integrated financial solution.

11. **Web site functionality.** The steps for finding information and then making informed decisions have to take less than two to three mouse clicks. Individuals who use *www.vanguard.com* will find it is easier finding information about their mutual funds on their Web site than going to their offices and trying to read through the mountains of fund prospectuses. Vanguard has been very smart in developing a system that asks users a series of

questions that helps them figure out what fund would fit their investment strategy. The information on the fund selected is written in plain English, which makes it easier for the buyer to make an informed and quick decision.

12. **Security.** What determines the success or failure of any transaction site is its ability to give the user a feeling of unbreakable security. This is especially true with online financial products. Users are always concerned that some smart computer hacker will get in and steal their money or private information.

Examples of Success

I chose Raging Bull (*www.ragingbull*), now a division of AltaVista (*www.altavista.com*), and Quotesmith.com (*www.quotesmith.com*) because they closely follow the above twelve elements.

From a user's standpoint, I selected Raging Bull because my wife, children, and I own a variety of stocks and I am interested in reading the discussion boards dedicated to various public companies. I have dumped stocks when I noticed that comments were running consistently negative. When one of my stocks is slumping, I will click on the information links to find out what the company has reported to the various regulatory bodies. Most of the people I know who buy stocks visit Raging Bull at least once a week, and when the market is doing well, they visit daily.

I firmly believe commodity-type financial products such as term life insurance and automotive insurance will be bought over the Internet. Companies like Quotesmith.com provide consumers with the ability to shop multiple insurance companies without having to be pressed by an insurance agent or broker into selecting the company she represents or the one that pays her the fattest commission check.

Below is a chart that provides insights into what it takes to build, maintain, and grow successful online financial services content and e-commerce business.

	Quotesmith.com	RagingBull.com
Initial cost to build Web site	$3 million plus	$1 million plus
Cost to maintain Web site	$2 million plus	$1 million plus
Full-time technologists/ content developers	24	20 plus
No. of salespeople/ business development	1	3 plus
Employee time commitment	40–50 hours per week	50–60 hours per week
Projected growth of sales department	3	Not disclosing
Biggest day-to-day concern	Customer satisfaction	Keeping content fresh
Marketing techniques	Print Radio Television Public relations Direct mail E-mail	E-mail newsletter Media coverage Word of mouth
Best marketing techniques	Print advertising	Word of mouth
Projected growth of marketing budget	$100 million	Not disclosing
Strategic partnerships	Zoom	AltaVista
Retention techniques	Quarterly newsletter	Community advocates

Quotesmith.com Interview

Three of Quotesmith.com's executives participated in this interview.

William V. Thoms has served as the executive vice president and chief operating officer since 1994. Willard L. Hemsworth II has served as senior vice president of marketing since November 1999. Hemsworth holds a BS in advertising communications from the

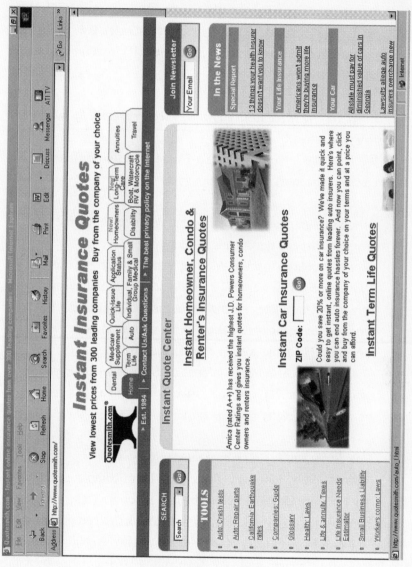

www.quotesmith.com

University of Illinois and an MBA in marketing management from Loyola University Chicago. Burke A. Christensen has served as vice president of operations and general counsel since January 1999. He is the coauthor and editor of two textbooks on insurance law. He holds a BS in history from Utah State University and a JD from the University of Utah College of Law.

What are the three to five critical success factors by which you measure yourselves?

We have the largest content. We have over 300 different insurance carriers. The most important things we focus on are:

- *Speed.* Our graphics aren't fancy, but we know they want to get to the quote fast and downloads will lose them.
- *Choice.* People go to a Wal-Mart for a large a variety of choices.
- *Convenience.* You want to be able to do it when you want to do it.
- *Accuracy.* Our quotes are always accurate. We provide the rating services for our carrier. We don't provide advice. The rating service will help the consumer make a decision.
- *Control.* The customer is in control. Some sites refer you to an agent. With our site, you don't have to speak to a sales agent. You are working directly with the carrier.

How important is first mover advantage?

It is extremely important. There are a lot of companies out there that reporters are doing articles about that reporters haven't done their homework on. We ask the reporters to ask our competitors how many policies have actually been sold. How many eyeballs that come to the site isn't meaningful. We have sold 40,000 policies over the last three years.

It takes three to nine months until people move on the quotes. They like to speak with family, accountants, and financial advisors.

Have you developed strategic partnerships and have they brought in new business?

The partnerships have worked well. It has been small and growing. If we sign an alliance partner today, it might take three months or longer to get them to sign. Some of our applications are twelve pages long and we are trying to overcome that. We just implemented Adobe technology that allows you to download forms, and some of your information will already be on the forms.

What does your organization do to retain users?

We send quarterly newsletters. Ninety-five percent of our business is in term life insurance. Most keep the policy for a year. Only 2 percent drop in a year. By allowing them to find what they need at the price they want to pay. Since we aren't trying to persuade them, they don't think we are pushing them into anything they don't want or need.

What unique approaches are you using to retain employees?

We have stock options, we pay them well, and the place is on fire. We have ice cream distributed and we feed them well. Our benefits package is very good.

What new technologies do you plan to deploy to make the user experience better that will result in more users?

Giving the customer the ability to download the application at home makes the process easier and more accurate. We look forward to when people can digitally alter applications on the screen. The goal is to drag the nineteenth-century paper part of the industry into twenty-first century e-commerce.

What technologies do you think are overrated?

The instant quotes that our competitors promote are overrated. Few of them live up to the hype. There is not one company that has the lowest prices for different ages. The Internet shopper is not going to overpay for insurance.

What didn't you expect that turned out well?

What we are doing today, we didn't expect to do when we got started. We didn't sit down and say we are going to sell insurance nationally from one place. I sat through many industry seminars and strategic planning sessions and no one came up with the idea that is Quotesmith.com today. The concept has evolved over time.

What didn't you expect that didn't turn out well?

We thought banner ads were pretty cool, but we didn't have any real success with banner ads.

Raging Bull Interview

Stephen J. Killeen is president and CEO of Raging Bull, spearheading brand expansion and managing strategic development. Stephen assumes leadership of Raging Bull as a ten-year veteran of online financial services. Most recently, he helped establish and grow Fidelity Investments' online trading capability, bringing the financial services giant to the number two position behind Charles Schwab. On his departure, Fidelity boasted 2 million online accounts, 30,000 online trades per day, and more than $100 billion in assets managed. Stephen received a BA in political science from Union College, Schenectady, New York, in 1984.

How will your business model survive long term?

In the past year we have aggressively added content and tools to our site to increase the value we bring to our users. As part of the AltaVista network, we can accelerate the pace of development and volume of content on the site.

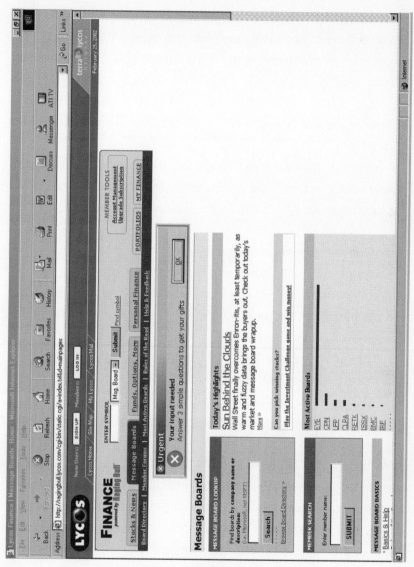

ragingbull.lycos.com

AltaVista can leverage our strength in finance to become the most comprehensive financial destination on the Internet. In addition, AltaVista can take advantage of our strength in the community to build communities not just in finance, but also across their network, for people who are passionate about travel, sports, politics, and a variety of other areas.

What are the critical success factors from a technology point of view?

We are committed to achieving the maximum performance and uptime so our members are always guaranteed fast, reliable access to the information they rely on to make investing decisions.

What are the critical design factors?

Our site fulfills the promise of the Internet by connecting millions of people around the world in a forum where they can share their ideas and passions. With this in mind, the site is designed with two priorities: speed and community.

The site is "built for speed." Regardless of an individual system's access speed, Raging Bull is designed to provide a quick, helpful, and intuitive experience for the consumer.

Raging Bull is also designed to facilitate and build the community. Our goal is to navigate visitors into the message boards that comprise the Raging Bull community and engage them so that they become active and consistent participants in the community. We make all of our design decisions based on a single criterion: "How does this enhance the community?" To that end, we make the member the center of the universe by featuring members' best posts and most popular boards on our home page. In every instance, there is a call to join the discussion, to challenge another member's ideas, or to offer an opinion on a breaking news event.

What are the critical marketing factors to driving people to your Web site?

Viral growth has been our most effective means of growing the site. Raging Bull's members are passionate about investing. They are also passionate about the community. They feel a sense of ownership because they are posting their own thoughts on the boards. As a result, they take pride in inviting their friends and colleagues to join.

We also have received great media coverage. In the summer of 1998, when Jason Anders at the Wall Street Journal Interactive Edition first covered the site, we saw a dramatic spike in membership and page views. Today, we are regularly featured among listings of the top Web site picks in major personal finance and business magazines. Every time we receive good coverage, our Web site traffic and membership accelerate considerably.

Until October 1999, we didn't spend any money on marketing except for the investment in some Raging Bull T-shirts, hats, and bumper stickers. We have been able to grow the community to more than 350,000 members and more than 7 million page views on a trading day, based purely on the organic growth that comes from the click of a mouse and from public relations.

What future technologies have you seen that can revolutionize the way people share and obtain information?

The technologies like instant messaging and Web-to-wireless messaging that are currently accelerating in adoption and refinement will increase the already rapid pace of information dissemination. It will become more and more common to see people conducting stock trades through their pager on the beach or ordering a new putter through a PDA just after they wrapped the old one around a tree after a bad putt at the golf course.

Broadband also can dramatically change the way people access and share information. As more and more people get connected over high-speed networks, not only will they be able to use existing sites quickly and efficiently, but they'll be able to use communications technologies featuring sound, voice, and video to further enhance their communications. Far-reaching high-speed access also allows for more media-rich sites, more dynamic sites, and an Internet experience that will be appealing to and accessible for the general public.

Is it better to change the interface that people are used to dealing with every couple of years or keep it the same because there is a degree of comfort with things one is used to?

There's not a black-and-white answer to that question. We are constantly looking for ways to make our site more appealing and easy-to use. If we learned that a site redesign would be received well by our current members and add value to the community, then we would certainly redesign. Consumers are open to change as long as it benefits them. To redesign just for the sake of shaking things up, however, is likely to disenchant our users.

What is the future of online financial services?

Insurance, stock brokerage, and business information are a perfect fit for the Internet because the Internet is instantaneous and its products don't have to be built, wrapped, or shipped. The Internet allows people the ability to compare a variety of products at one time. The user has the power and is the gatekeeper and that is what the insurance and stockbroker used to do.

The Internet has the capacity to collect information faster and then produce a policy within a day. This will come through hooking up with your doctor's records and the state motor vehicle records. Companies like Quotesmith.com and regional independent insurance brokers that have their own Web sites won't care what policy you buy. They just care about providing choices, accuracy, and ease.

Chapter Summary

Anyone who is offering financial content and products for consumers has to focus on the following:

1. **Depth and integrity of information.** Today's online business consumers don't want to pay full commissions; therefore, they want the same level of information that their stockbroker and investment advisor receive so they can make their own decisions.

2. **Timeliness.** Today's online business consumers are checking their stock portfolio throughout the day. To make informed decisions, they need the latest information and insights from industry leaders and analysts.

3. **Choice.** Today's online consumers use the Internet because they want to comparison shop. The Web sites that don't provide numerous choices don't attract users.

4. **Quality of vendors.** Today's online consumers want to buy from names they can trust or from names that are trusted by organizations that they trust, such as Consumer Guide or Morningstar, the mutual fund rating service.

5. **Ability to purchase online.** Today's online consumers want to spend as little time with salespeople as possible and want to buy products at their convenience. Therefore, online stockbrokers and insurance companies need to be able to provide online forms and then the ability to purchase online once the appropriate legal documentation has been forwarded and filed.

6. **Customer service.** Today's online consumers don't want to have to go on a treasure hunt to find the telephone number of customer service or have to wait more than a couple of minutes for a live person to answer their questions.

7. **Smart use of technology.** Today's online consumers don't want to spend a lot of time downloading documents and information. Use technologies that are widely available such as Adobe Acrobat

for forms and audio for interviews. Until home users have cable modems or T-1 capability, stay away from video because it eats up too much memory and isn't reliable.

If you are a regional insurance broker, bank, or business publication, you should be leveraging the Internet to reduce costs and increase revenue. The Internet is the perfect medium for the financial services and business content business.

Chapter 9
Human Resource Service Sites

WHETHER THE ECONOMY IS GOOD OR BAD, HUMAN resources plays a continuous and important role. Companies are either in the process of hiring additional employees because demand for their product or service is great, or they are in the midst of letting go employees because demand has slackened or because mergers have resulted in numerous employees serving overlapping functions.

The two most popular types of human resource related sites are sites that provide career advice and sites that help employees find new jobs and employers find talented job candidates. Below is a chart that shows the large number of human resource related sites you would find by performing a search on Yahoo.com.

Word	No. of Categories	No. of Sites
Career advice	1	143
Career counseling	2	206
Employment recruiting	6	578
Jobs	20	5,983
Online training	2	640

The human resource category is becoming increasingly crowded. With a hot economy, companies are willing to advertise on national and regional employment sites. These same hot companies need assistance in training their young managers. Older employees who have made a career with past and current employers need advice on how to jumpstart their careers or move into untried professional waters.

Today's sellers and buyers of services gravitate to Web sites whose value proposition revolves around offering quality information and leveraging of technology. Human resource companies who traditionally increased staff to meet increased demand from clients now realize they can leverage the technology of the Web to cover a greater geographic area and don't need to add additional consultants to support their growth.

10 Keys to Online Human Resource Success

There are ten key elements to building a successful online human resource business:

1. **Career advice.** Technology and the Internet have completely changed people's career foci and goals. Traditionally, when college graduates left academia, they would look for one company to build their career with. In the 1980s and early 1990s, the concept of one job per career disappeared with merger mania. Now the Internet has come along and changed what skills and what types of companies professionals should focus on. It's become confusing, and people are looking for advice on how best to manage their careers and their personal lives. Companies like Right Management Consultants, *www.right.com*, the largest outplacement firm in the world, which is featured in this chapter, are influencing how experienced managers should position themselves in the new business order by having their career consultants provide advice online.

2. **Resume flow.** Technology companies and companies that are leveraging technology by creating Internet businesses are growing at such a rapid rate that they can't get enough qualified resumes to fill the demand. Web sites like *www.monster.com* are popular with national corporate recruiters because they drive traffic on a national basis, which saves companies money from running advertisements in major regional dailies. Local job sites, such as the one featured at the end of this chapter, *www.jobnet.com*, assist local companies with recruiting by reaching a younger, technology-driven audience and by providing instant response to advertisements.

3. **Resume construction.** All of the top job sites advise and assist employees in how to create resumes that will accentuate the positives of their careers and life experiences. Many sites, such as *www.jobs.com*, assist you in creating your resume and, once it is completed, send it out automatically to interested companies.

4. **Online job fairs.** Employers trying to hire technologists, salespeople, marketing people, and writers want to make their companies appear to be friendly but aggressive in terms of hiring quickly and focused on results that will increase stock option values and cash bonus opportunities. They participate in online job fairs, such as the one run by *www.jobnet.com*, so they can respond daily to potential recruits.

5. **Employee presentation.** Executive recruitment sites such as *www.kornferry.com* are starting to use video and audio so employers can get a better feel for the candidates before they meet them in person. The companies use video streaming technology and ask the candidate a series of general questions about themselves and their career. This is an extremely valuable screening tool, especially related to sales positions.

6. **Reading suggestions.** Companies like Right Management Consultants, *www.right.com*, and their competitor, Manchester

International, *www.manchesterus.com,* develop a list of books they have vetted and white papers they have internally created for both candidates and human resource professionals to go to for advice and insights into interviewing and recruiting. These firms are demonstrating and leveraging their knowledge base to build a rapport with both the buyer and the seller so they can capture additional business in executive coaching and employment recruiting.

7. **Salary surveys.** People who are currently employed or who are looking for new opportunities want to know what the market thinks they are worth. A staple of the top employment sites, such as *www.headhunter.net,* is providing salary information so candidates know what to ask for and expect from employers.

8. **Networking.** Job sites such as *www.monsterboard.com* are bringing together recruiters and prospects online through chat rooms that are sponsored by a particular company. They are also developing chat rooms for prospects to compare notes with each other.

9. **Entrepreneurial advice.** Over the past ten years, there has been a growing trend for people to take more control of their lives by starting their own companies. Those companies range from one-man consultancies to venture-backed businesses. Outplacement firms such as Lee Hecht Harrison, *www.lhh.com*, and Drake Beam Morin, *www.dbm.com*, understand that many of their future clients will come from the ranks of the unemployed. Therefore, they provide advice from entrepreneurs and links to sites that assist entrepreneurs in building their business.

10. **Executive coaching.** Young executives and their employers are looking for seasoned professionals to assist them in developing their management skills. Because companies are so busy growing, they don't have time to send their people to management seminars, so they need to interact with a coach on their

own time. The executive coaching and outplacement firms are starting to make the transition from in-person to online support.

Examples of Success

Although human resource companies receive their revenue from corporations, their audience is predominantly individuals who are primarily using their home computers. The two examples of human resource oriented sites that are included here smartly incorporate a good balance of information and services and deliver the information in a way that encourages home users to bookmark their sites.

The first example, Right Management Consultants, is the worldwide leader in outplacement. It was an early adopter in developing a Web site and has continued to leverage the Web to provide services for its clients. Clients now count on Right's ability to deliver meaningful content to its current and former employees through the Web.

The second example, JOBNET.com, was developed for the Internet. It realized that college students with technology degrees would more likely use the Internet to find opportunities than they would their local newspaper. It also realized that, as the Internet grew, companies would see that the best way to attract college graduates would be to put their employment needs online and recruit online. The site isn't graphically exciting, but when you speak with corporate recruiters, you find that it is still very effective.

The following is a chart that shows you the differences in tactics and focus between an existing bricks-and-mortar traditional human resources company using the Internet to attract and retain clients and a Web-based human resources company that uses the Internet to attract and retain traditional and nontraditional companies.

	Right Management Consultants	JOBNET
Initial cost to build Web site	$100,000 plus	$50,000
Cost to maintain Web site	$25,000 plus per year	$36,000 per year
Full-time technologists/ content developers	4 part time	7
No. of salespeople	None	6
Employee time commitment	50 hours per week	30–50 hours per week
Projected growth of sales department	None	None
Biggest day-to-day concern	Optimum use by clients and employees	
Marketing techniques	Postcards Business cards Stationery Marketing materials	Print advertising E-mail Public events Telemarketing Links Cable television Billboard Web
Best marketing techniques	Face-to-face meetings	Public events Web Cable television
Projected growth of marketing budget	Very little	Same
Strategic partnerships	None	National job sites Advertising agencies

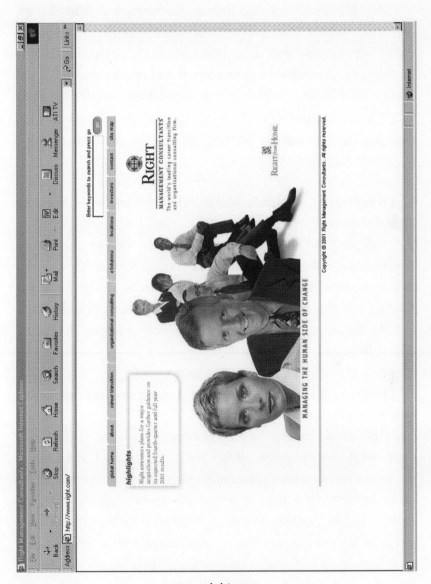

www.right.com

Right Management Consultants Interview

Robin Mickelson is the Interactive Services and Marketing Manager for Right Management Consultants, a career transition and consulting company with more than 200 offices worldwide. In this capacity, she oversees the development and maintenance of all of Right's Web services, which include support services for the company's career management and consulting capabilities. In addition, she manages Right's image and branding efforts. She graduated from the University of Minnesota.

What type of financial commitment does it take to build a successful Web site?

It depends on the strategies that you are trying to accomplish; whether you are looking to have interactivity; whether you are hosting it yourself or not (e.g., do you need to buy hardware?); and whether you plan on creating a marketing campaign to support the site. It can be anywhere from a few thousand to a few hundred thousand dollars.

What size of financial commitment should a company be thinking of to maintain its site?

Again, it depends on the goals of the site. If content will be added daily, weekly, or monthly, obviously it takes money and/or time resources to create content, and that should be planned for accordingly. However, even if the site will not have frequent content additions, a monthly budget should be planned to ensure that the site is updated on a regular basis. Even sites that are just designed to be informational about a company will need to have regular updates to keep the site current—from posting press releases, to updating executive bios, to adding product information.

What are the three to five critical success factors you measure yourselves by?

1. Did we meet our strategy/goal that we set for the Web site?
2. Is the Web site suitable for our audience/client?
3. Is the Web site easy to use and navigate?
4. Is the content updated, relevant, and accurate?
5. Is everything working and operational?

What is your biggest day-to-day concern?

We have several Web sites. We have one that is purely for marketing, and others that are designed for client-specific purposes. All of our sites are designed to meet career-related needs of our individual and corporate clients. My biggest day-to-day concern is that our internal employees understand the differences between them, know how to use them, and know how to describe them appropriately to our clients.

How important is first mover advantage?

Important, but it depends on your business strategy. In some instances, what works for another company just won't work for you, so being first is not relevant. You need to make sure that the Web solutions that you create make sense and are aligned with your business strategy.

What does your organization do to retain users?

Our users are utilizing our services, and the Web service is a core component of the service delivery, so we don't have any challenges with retention issues.

What is the most difficult part of retaining users?

We do focus on keeping the site content fresh and up to date. If it becomes stale and dated, the site will be ineffective.

What unique approaches are you using to retain employees?

Unlike a startup company, we are well established and a leader in our field, so we don't feel the need to come up with unusual approaches. We are already a public company, so most people get stock options or the ability to buy their stock through a 401K. We have a great health benefits package.

What is unique about your site that makes users want to bookmark it?

Of our sites, we have one that is designed primarily as an informational site about us. We have not employed strategies to make it a bookmarked site.

What didn't you expect that turned out well?

Being fairly new to Web project management, it was amazing to me how many things we needed to test in different browsers, applications, et cetera before we launched our site. We planned on the testing, but I did not expect some of the kinds of errors that we encountered. Using an apostrophe, for instance, in the body of a message posted to our "eMessage Center" caused an error, which we had to fix. Everything turned out fine, it was just surprising the range of details we had to focus on in order to make the site function perfectly under all circumstances.

What didn't you expect that didn't turn out well?

In working with several vendors that provide services through our site to our clients, I was surprised at how difficult it is to work with some companies—misinformation provided by these vendors ended up making the process more complicated and cumbersome than it needed to be.

JOBNET Interview

Ward Christman is the founder and president of Malvern, Pennsylvania-based JOBNET.com, Inc., the parent company of the

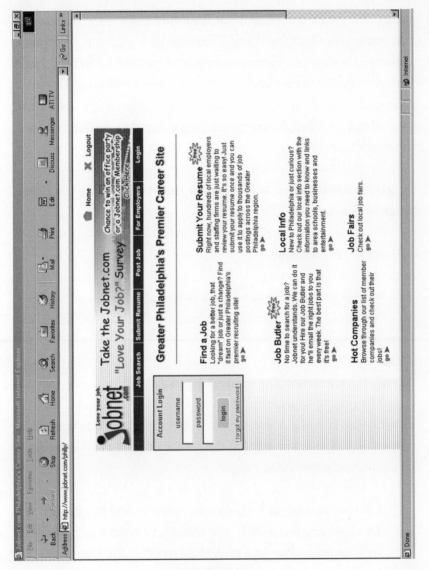

www.jobnet.com

Internet's *www.jobnet.com*, a regional online job and resume service. Since 1992, he has formed alliances with national and local recruitment sites, media outlets, and job fairs to help job seekers find jobs and employers find candidates. Christman is a graduate of Widener University with an engineering degree, and participates in many local human resources organizations such as Society for Human Resources Management and National Human Resources Association. As an avid user of the Internet, he enjoys mixing computers with the human aspects of recruiting.

What are the three to five critical success factors by which you measure yourselves?
Customer renewals, profitability, hires, growth (public and corporate users), growth (sales).

What is your biggest day-to-day concern?
Enhancing our content and technology to make our site user-friendlier.

How important is first mover advantage?
Being the first mover in a market is extremely important, because everyone is striving to come up with a cool, new service to entice customers. Having the service that the customer wants first establishes credibility and captures the market.

Will your marketing budget go up over the next five years?
Our marketing budget will increase as we continue to grow; however, we base the budget on a percentage of sales, and that percentage is not likely to change with growth.

Do you have an affiliates program, and how has it worked?
We have some affiliate programs with advertising agencies to

sell our services for a commission. Overall, the program has worked, but we have to constantly educate the individual account executives and persuade them on the benefits our services can provide their clients. It requires a lot of manpower and time to make the programs successful.

Have you developed strategic partnerships and have they brought in new business?

JOBNET.com partners with national employment sites in order to sell their services to regional companies, for a commission. These partnerships account for approximately 15 percent of our revenues. We use these partnerships to create credibility and establish name recognition for our new prospects.

We also partner with cable television and radio groups for cobranding event advertising. Both partnerships have brought in new business and sales leads. Equally important to the revenue produced through the partnerships are the increased brand awareness created through advertising on television and the radio.

What does your organization do to retain users?

Running an employment site means we need to constantly add new job postings, new resumes, and new companies for the job seekers and employers who visit our site. JOBNET.com is updated every day with this new information. Employers receive a daily listing via e-mail of all new resumes in the database, and job seekers receive an e-mail on a weekly basis with the new jobs that match their specified skill category and location.

What is the most difficult part of retaining users?

The most difficult part of retaining users is getting the users to take full advantage of the service once they pay for it. If they do not use the service to its fullest, they won't renew. For job seekers, once they find a new job or stop actively looking for a job, they aren't going to visit our site.

What unique approaches are you using to retain employees?

I try to remain flexible and accommodate their needs. Since it is a small company, I give people a certain level of autonomy to do their jobs. I also encourage my employees to attend seminars and training sessions.

What is unique about your site that makes users want to book-mark it?

We update the open jobs database each day. An active job seeker should bookmark the site so he or she can check to see what new jobs have been posted and apply for the jobs he or she is interested in before the job has been filled.

What new technologies do you plan to deploy to make the user experience better that will result in more users?

We will be using active server- and database-driven technology—XML and DHTML—to enhance the site. Providing a dynamic site with content that's important to the users will keep them coming back to the site and telling their friends about their good experience.

What didn't you expect that turned out well?

I didn't expect our industry to become "mainstream" so quickly. Now that most job seekers and employers are using the Web to recruit, our business has skyrocketed.

What didn't you expect that didn't turn out well?

I didn't expect that some companies would buy the service and then not use it to its fullest capabilities.

Chapter Summary

To develop a successful human resource site, you have to focus primarily in five areas:

1. **Quality of information.** The information can't be shallow and brochurelike. It has to make a statement that the company has a deep understanding of how to solve management problems and improve individual performance.
2. **Interactivity.** Users want to interact with management consultants and business leaders to get insights and advice in order to move their careers and companies forward.
3. **Resume assistance.** There must be the ability to develop quality resumes to improve the users' chances of finding better opportunities.
4. **Employment opportunities.** Users want to see what new opportunities are available, and they want to be able to immediately seize the opportunity.
5. **Exchanging ideas.** Providing an online forum through chat rooms allows users to exchange ideas.

Chapter 10
Entertainment

ACCORDING TO NIELSEN//NETRATINGS Audience Measurement Service report on October 14, 2001, individuals are currently visiting the Internet six times a week and spending 18 hours a month on the Internet. What that statistic tells us is that Americans are watching television less and turning to the Internet for news and entertainment. Below is a chart based on a search on Yahoo! I did related to entertainment-type Web sites. You will notice that there are over 1,700 categories and over 43,000 Web sites related to entertainment. This includes everything from online video games to online game shows to online entertainment publications, sports, and sweepstakes.

Word	No. of Categories	No. of Sites
Entertainment	56	9,034
Gambling	15	1,819
Games	236	14,089
Game shows	134	489
Sports	113	19,813
Sweepstakes	1	10,800

Value for User

Entertainment was one of the major reasons the Internet gained traction with consumers. Consumers were looking for alternative forms of inexpensive, relaxing fun outside of watching television. Online entertainment has taken off because of the following five reasons:

- It's interactive.
- It's mentally challenging.
- There are no day or time restrictions to participate.
- There is an opportunity to win prizes.
- It helps to reduce stress.

Value for Advertiser

U.S. online ad spending will reach $5.4 billion, up from $2.8 billion last year, according to Forrester Research. A large part of those advertising dollars is spent with companies similar to those discussed later in this chapter—Bikini.com, Boxerjam, and Webstakes.com. There are three reasons advertisers flock to entertainment sites:

- *One-on-one marketing.* The advertiser can develop a relationship with the user because sites like Webstakes.com customize their home pages for their users based on the users' taste. If the advertiser knows what the user is interested in, then it can focus its product and service offerings.
- *Demographic information.* Entertainment sites require their players to fill out information about themselves such as their age and where they live. This is manna from heaven for direct marketers who want to pinpoint potential buyers of their clients' products and services.
- *Inexpensive advertising costs.* Entertainment companies typically charge advertisers for the number of users that click on their

banner advertisements. The value in this is that you pay only for people who are truly interested, and you know who is using the site by the demographic information supplied by the site.

10 Tactics to Use to Build a Successful Entertainment Site

Each of the companies featured in this chapter has over 1 million unique visitors who come to their Web site each month. There are ten tactics you can use to build a successful entertainment site.

1. **Create excitement.** Entertainment is all about getting people excited and foaming at the mouth to participate. The best entertainment Web sites pulsate with excitement by showing a lot of activity and giving users a sense that they are part of a big party or game show. They accomplish this through a combination of animation, large cash prizes, real-time competition, and interaction with famous people through chat rooms. Go to *www.iwon.com* and what is your eye attracted to? It is attracted to the top of the page that beckons you to enter daily, monthly, and yearly contests where the cash prizes range from $10,000 to $10 million. When you visit *www.webstakes.com,* which is featured in this chapter, you will be attracted to the variety of prizes.

2. **Offer creative content.** The content has to be unique. I was at a venture capital conference at which the founders of *www.bikini.com*, were presenting. Everyone who went to view their site said they felt like they were on an island attending a beach party. The visitor to the site sees young people dancing and having a great time and puts the users in a fun frame of mind.

3. **Include exciting graphics.** Fun graphics put the visitor in a carefree mood to give personal information and spend money. My daughters love *www.nick.com* because, as my eleven-year-old

puts it, the "graphics are cool." They are so inviting that she goes to the site every day and plays games and they poll kids are various topics such as what cartoon character should run for mayor. In this way, the site promotes viewership; my daughter wants to watch the various shows to see if they ask her question.

4. **Keep it fresh.** Manufacturing and other slow-to-change product introduction Web sites can get by updating sites quarterly or, at most, monthly. The graphics of sites for industries that don't rely on people visiting their Web sites every day may be able to update their sites as little as once every other year, and still have an effective site. However, in the entertainment world, the latest technology, new content, and stylish graphics have to be applied on a continuous basis. Look at the *www.boxerjam.com* home page and you will see that new games are added on a weekly basis.

5. **Ensure quick download.** Because most of the users of entertainment sites are using home computers and modems whose speeds aren't above 56K, you have to be careful about the size and amount of pictures you use. Large graphic files tend to slow the download time of a site to a crawl. This limitation should become irrelevant over the next two years, as cable modems and ISDN or DSL connections come down in cost. But, for now, slow downloads mean waving good-bye to potential visitors. Once you lose them, they are hard to bring back.

6. **Capture demographic information.** Unlike any other medium where the interaction is one way, advertisers and sponsors love entertainment sites because in order to win prizes and receive free newsletters, users typically have to provide information about themselves.

7. **Include newsletters.** Good entertainment sites have newsletters that promote weekly changes in the site and discuss companies that are sponsoring individual sections and prizes on the site.

This builds visibility for the site and the sponsor, and reminds the user to come back to visit because the fun is ongoing.

8. **Tout winners.** The best entertainment sites let the user know that it is possible to win by posting the first initial, the last name, and the state of different winners each day. The sites are careful to guard the privacy of the winners, but at the same time, potential players need to be reassured that there are winners. Webstakes.com promotes its winners right on its home page.

9. **Form partnerships.** When the Internet was relatively new, providing entertainment for a specific demographic or developing games for different demographics and selling advertising targeted to each demographic was enough to bring in steady revenue. Today, entertainment sites have to position themselves as a tool for client retention.

10. **Understand the user.** There are a lot of great 3-D graphics and other types of technology that would make playing games on the Internet even more exciting. Unfortunately, 90 percent of Internet users still use a dial-up connection, which means their modem speeds will not allow them to fully use 3-D and full-motion video in a way that will not cripple their systems. The companies who want to use technology that is slow to download should look to partner with companies such as Excite-At Home that sell cable modems, and offer their products as premium add-ons to these services. They could charge fees similar to cable channels.

Examples of Success

I believe entertainment Web sites are going to be huge beneficiaries of the Internet because of high-speed cable access, which will proliferate throughout the United States and many of the other major countries throughout the world. Within five to ten years, every television will have the ability to connect to the Internet, and that means that entertainment sites will allow their customers to play each other live and in real time. You won't be watching *Who Wants to Be a Millionaire?*, because you will be able to pay a fee and play with millions of other viewers.

I have interviewed two company executives who I think best understand how to build a fun and entertaining Web site and at the same time understand how to use entertainment as a way to attract and keep users, to deliver a corporate message, and to make money. Below is a chart that gives you insights into what it costs to build their Web sites, maintain them, and grow them into successful businesses.

	Boxerjam	Webstakes.com
Initial cost to build Web site	Less than $1 million	$500,000–$1 million
Cost to maintain Web site	$2 million	$2–$5 million
Full-time technologists/ content developers	30	50
No. of salespeople	5	30
Projected growth of sales department	15%	Double
Employee time commitment	40–50 hours per week	50 hours per week
Biggest day-to-day concern	Competition	Meeting objectives
Marketing techniques	Distribution partners E-mail Public relations	Strategic partners Opt-in e-mail Public relations
Best marketing techniques	Word of mouth Distribution partners	Opt-in e-mail Strategic partnerships
Strategic partnerships	Yahoo! AOL	NBC Hollywood stock exchange Excite

Boxerjam Interview

Allen A. Cunningham, president and CEO, began his professional career in information services at Morgan Stanley & Co., Inc., in New York. Among other projects, he was responsible for the development of systems for the firm's leveraged buyout and real estate funds. Prior to founding Boxerjam, Cunningham was the CFO of The Portofino Group, Inc., a real-estate development company located in Miami, Florida. He graduated from the University of Virginia in 1987 with a BA in English.

What do you need to provide users to make a successful community site?

You have to give people tools to interact and communicate with each other. Then you must provide a context for interaction, which is generally a shared interest of some sort, such as sports, stocks, parenting, music, et cetera. In our case, the context is games, and the interaction between people is in the games themselves, which makes them a particularly compelling programming vehicle.

How do you find out what your potential users want out of an online community?

You have to ask them. Nothing helps engender community more than giving people a vehicle to provide input. We didn't test-market an idea and build it. We built what we thought people would like and hoped they would come. Our users tell us ways in which we can improve the experience. We get thousands of e-mails each month with feedback ranging from comments on graphics and suggestions for prizes, to ideas for new game features.

What are the three to five critical success factors by which you measure yourselves?

We measure ourselves by the quality of our product, how many people enjoy the product, and how often they return. Conversion rates,

www.boxerjam.com

retention rates, and the number of monthly unique users are the key metrics. The product has to be the very best.

How important is first mover advantage?

Huge! If you are not the leader in the category, then you want to be within striking distance. If you are a startup, you have to assume that a group of big companies will want to be in your business. Being early gives you an opportunity for leadership despite where the big guys are. You have to spend a lot less money if you are early.

Which marketing techniques have worked the best?

Our most effective and lowest-cost marketing technique is having people tell other people. Next to that, our distribution partners have worked the best.

When we started, word of mouth was the primary traffic driver. Now it's distribution partnerships. Word of mouth isn't sustainable unless you have the hottest idea going, like an eBay.

Do you have an affiliates program, and how has it worked?

We do not have an affiliates program, but we are looking at it. There are a number of issues, such as control of the user data and the Media Metrics credit, that we need to sort out.

Have you developed strategic partnerships and have they brought in new business?

The distribution partnerships we have with AOL and Yahoo! have been great. We basically built our business on AOL, starting with them in 1995. Now we have a very substantial Web presence and now half our daily traffic comes from the Web. We have up to 150,000 players daily, and we are approaching 2 million users per month.

What does your organization do to retain users?

We retain users by giving them a fun, entertaining experience. Our games are fun. Since people can chat with each other during the games, they are particularly effective at building community. Among other things, we also feature high scorers, prizes, and newsletters in our site programming.

What is the most difficult part of retaining users?

There are so many choices out there and so many companies competing for people's time. Maintaining mind-share with the user is a challenge.

What unique approaches are you using to retain employees?

We have been in our business for a while, and early on, we focused on creating an environment that was fun and enjoyable. Everything we do is effectively new. There is innovation every day. Our employees enjoy this. They also get a lot of satisfaction from the number of people that come to the site and enjoy what we do. The potential financial rewards of stock options are obviously attractive, but the other stuff has to be there first. We are lucky we are in Charlottesville, Virginia, where we don't have a lot of competition from other companies trying to get our employees.

We are careful not to burn people out. You spend so much time and money building intellectual capital in your employees and you don't want them to leave. I don't think working harder is the answer. I think you need to work smarter and come up with more innovative product. That is how you retain employees. Having a balanced life is important.

What is unique about your site that makes users want to bookmark it?

The entertainment we offer is all original. You can't find it anywhere else. It's fun for the whole family. We offer a complete entertainment experience that you can get in 12 to 15 minutes, day in and day out.

What new technologies do you plan to deploy to make the user experience better that will result in more users?

We need to develop ways for users to get into our games faster. We look forward to the capabilities brought about by broadband and the set-top box. All of our technology planning is headed in that direction.

What didn't you expect that turned out well?

A couple of years ago when we were looking for venture capital, it was difficult because we weren't near the traditional venture capital centers. It turned out that where we were located was very attractive to venture capitalists because of our ability to attract and retain employees. Charlottesville is a university town and people like to live here. We do not have the intense competition for employees found in places like San Francisco and New York.

What didn't you expect that didn't turn out well?

I didn't think it would take as long for Java to come around. Java is a great solution for game-based products because it allows high ease of entry into games in a browser-based environment. Unfortunately, it has taken Java a while to adequately support graphics and sound on which our branded game content depends. Different browser versions have also been a problem. Java has incredible promise and is an awesome language, but I thought it would happen faster.

What is the future of your industry on the Internet?

The online entertainment category is particularly exciting because it has yet to transfer to the television or interactive set-top box device. Television is the entertainment vehicle in the house, and interactive entertainment through the TV is going to be incredibly popular. Our industry, more than any other, will benefit from convergence because of the inherent nature of television as an entertainment device. You will click to our channel like you would Nick or HBO.

Webstakes.com Interview

Unity Stoakes is responsible for developing and managing all of the company's marketing and communications strategy, including advertising, public relations, investor relations, and trade marketing. Prior to Promotions.com (where he was the director of communications), he was the director of interactive marketing at Middleberg & Associates, a New York public relations agency, where he worked with companies such as CDnow, Datek Online, CBS MarketWatch, TheStreet.com, Multex Investor Network, Red Sky Interactive, and Wit Capital. Stoakes is a graduate of Boston University's prestigious Collaborative Degree Program, in which he earned a BS in mass communications and public relations and a BA in political science.

What are the three to five critical success factors you measure yourselves by?

The five factors that come to mind immediately are:

1. Reach
2. Promotional transactions
3. Members
4. Unique visitors
5. Revenue

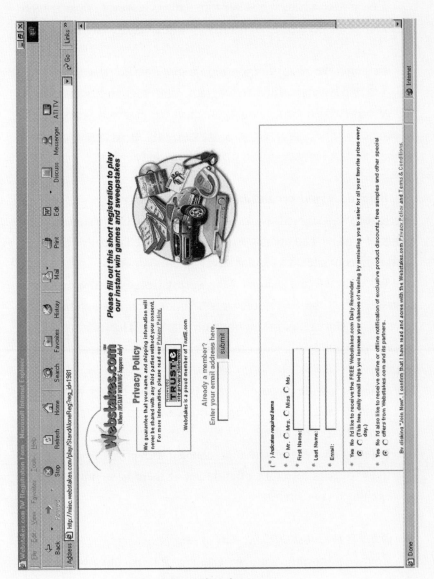

misc.webstakes.com

How important is first mover advantage?

First mover advantage is very important; however, what is more important is the perception of leadership within any given market.

Do you have an affiliates program and how has it worked?

Yes, we have an affiliates program. Our program began in 1997. We've experienced tremendous growth in the past two years. At the outset, our affiliates program was drawing fifty or so new members a week. Now that number is well over 1,000 weekly.

What does your organization do to retain users?

Effective, targeted use of our weekly e-mail newsletter, daily reminder e-mails, and theme-/event-related targeted e-mails keep users returning to our site on a regular basis.

We've also found success with sweepstakes designed where, once a person enters, he or she receives additional entries automatically when he or she enters promotions on our site. That method drives repeat traffic quite well. Other incentives for repeat use are:

1. Offering a wide range of prizes, promotions, instant win games, contests, and special offers in order to keep the site fresh and appeal to repeat visitors.
2. Offering a variety of activities, coupled with prizes, to give incentives to users to return often to see if there is anything new or exciting on our site.

What is the most difficult part of retaining users?

Continuing to produce new, exciting, and inventive promotions. The process is not difficult; we see it as a challenge.

What is unique about your site that makes users want to book-mark it?

We present a very large selection of promotions, prizes, special offers, and targeted content all in one place, including a listing of sweepstakes, Internet-wide.

What new technologies do you plan to deploy to make the user experience better that will result in more users?

We have and are constantly building a full suite of promotional products like Instant Win, Scavenger Hunt, and Lucky E-mail, to continue to provide new and exciting products to users/members.

What didn't you expect that turned out well?

We didn't expect the industry to be adopted so quickly by Fortune 500 companies.

What didn't you expect that didn't turn out well?

We also didn't expect the proliferation of bogus Internet business models and all of the clutter that has followed.

What is the future of your industry on the Internet?

First of all, we feel that the major media companies will dominate the Internet. As for the future of our industry, we will see a paradigm shift in offline marketing dollars moving online as well as in where the marketing dollars will be directed. Promotions and direct marketing will surpass traditional advertising within the next five years as a result of the Internet.

Chapter Summary

Unlike a lot of businesses on the Internet, for which there will be only a few winners, entertainment provides a multitude of opportunities and is a business that can't be dominated like Amazon.com does with books. The keys to building a successful entertainment model are:

1. **Database development.** Develop a site that solicits information about users, so advertisers and sponsors will see the value of partnering with your site.

2. **Interactivity.** Develop games and activities such as live chat with famous people, so users feel the excitement of participation.

3. **Interesting content.** Develop content that is fun and interesting and creates a fantasy world for the user.

4. **Secure environment.** Develop a secure environment so users don't think someone will take their information and sell it to someone else.

Chapter 11
B2B Market Sites

ONE-FOURTH OF ALL U.S. B2B PURCHASING will be done online by the year 2003, according to a study by The Boston Consulting Group (*www.bcg.com*). The research estimates that over the next few years, U.S. B2B e-commerce will grow by 33 percent each year and reach $2.8 trillion in transaction value.

According to Charles Phillips, a managing director at Morgan Stanley and one of Wall Street's premier Internet analysts, within ten years, 100 percent of the gross domestic product will come from the Internet. The fastest-growing area in the B2B market will be with companies that set up marketplaces for buyers and sellers to get together on a global and, in some cases, regional basis. In a presentation made at the Mid-Atlantic Venture Capital Conference in Washington, D.C., Phillips outlined the value of online exchanges for buyers and sellers.

The Power of B2B

The reason B2B markets will be huge home runs is because they provide both buyers and sellers with substantial benefits.

Value for the Buyer	Value for the Seller
Price transparency	Aggregation of small orders
Variations in prices by region	Centralized market
Pricing better online than offline	Lower customer acquisition costs
Availability transparency	Larger orders
Ability to find out product availability	Network effect benefit
Supplier transparency	Competitive advantage will be discovered more quickly
Ability to find other suppliers	Lowers the cost servicing customers
Product transparency	Efficiencies in planning production and hiring
Ability to find substitutes and alternatives	Efficiencies in employment recruiting mechanism

How to Build a Successful Business Exchange

Every electronic commerce site requires an easy-to-use and easy-to-navigate home page connected to a well-structured database supported by a boatload of advertising and publicity. To build a successful business exchange, you have to involve everyone who would participate in the exchange to provide his or her thoughts and insights. You need to interview the buyers and sellers and find out what kinds of substantive information would encourage them to use the exchange and what would preclude them from using your exchange.

Business Exchange Killers

One of my clients operates an exchange in the printing industry. According to the 25 executives we interviewed, there were three reasons a buyer or seller would avoid getting involved with a business exchange.

1. **Too much competition.** Vendors don't mind competition, but they don't want to be pitted against the entire world. They especially don't want to be involved with companies that only claim to provide the same services or quality of services. Most vendors want to be able to interface with the customers and develop long-term relationships. Therefore, they would rather receive sales leads for companies within driving distance of their offices. Vendors realize they have to provide a competitive fair price, but they can't afford to have their margins squeezed to the point where they lose money on a contract.

2. **Poor proposal information.** The information found in the proposal will determine the vendor's response. Many business exchanges offer simplistic online proposal applications in an attempt to ensure that buyers will fill them out. The problem is that the vendor doesn't receive adequate information and therefore can't provide a realistic response. This forces the buyers and sellers to do so much extra work that they wonder why they need the exchange in the first place.

3. **Low price/low quality.** For example, some salespeople, in order to generate sales, will tell a buyer that they can do something that they don't really have the experience or capability to do in-house, just to generate commissions. By the time the buyer finds out that the vendor can't deliver what was agreed upon, the buyer ends up paying more to fix the problem and is left with a negative impression of the vendors involved in the exchange.

12 Elements of a Successful Business Exchange

The business exchanges that have the greatest chances of succeeding are sensitive to the above issues and contain the following twelve ingredients that will make them a success over the long term.

1. **Industry executives.** The competition in the B2B market space is growing so quickly that you need to hire executives and sales professionals with strong industry contacts. Strong industry contacts make it easier to raise money and shorten the sales cycle.

2. **Lots of capital.** The companies that raise the most capital and have the ability to bombard their audience with direct mail, e-mail, and advertising in industry publications will increase their chances of owning the market space they are playing in. As I am writing this book, the public market has basically shut out Internet content and e-commerce companies from obtaining capital. Therefore, you have to proceed as if you won't raise another dollar until revenue followed by profits validates your concept.

3. **First mover.** Don't waste your time starting an e-commerce business if you are the fourth or fifth company in a particular market space. In this chapter we feature VerticalNet, which has a market capitalization of over $5 billion and has developed business exchanges for over fifty markets. One of my clients had a better product than the first mover, but over 100 venture funds turned my client down. The venture funds contended that the cost to displace the number one company outweighed my client's potential profits.

4. **Media awareness.** Media awareness scares off potential investors who might be influenced to invest in your competition instead. Some companies have a difficult time raising money because the markets they want to get into are populated with well-known companies such as VerticalNet, which has received a tremendous amount of media exposure. The media attention given to VerticalNet resulted in successful companies such as Microsoft investing $100 million in VerticalNet.

5. **A win-win situation.** All of the business exchanges focus on providing the buyer the opportunity to purchase products and services at the lowest price and provide sellers a larger base of potential clients. In theory it sounds like a win-win situation, but

it has been my experience from working with companies in every field that the buyer comes out ahead on price and the sellers who participate end up with little or no profit. The exchanges that make sure the buyer saves money and the seller makes a profit will ensure themselves of long-term success. Exchanges who force 90 percent of their sellers out of business over time will cease to exist because the winners will eventually tell the exchange that they don't need them anymore.

6. **Directory/searching.** The search engine on an exchange has to be able to understand natural language questions. A smart exchange will test the site with non-technical people and have them enter in the queries that they would typically use to find information.

7. **Security technology.** Every day you read about breaches in security on the Internet and privacy issues. The sites that make a serious commitment to security will develop lasting relationships. Don't underestimate the importance of quality security.

8. **Customer service.** Buyers and sellers need to exchange official records if there are disagreements over transactions. They also need access to databases that provide information about both buyers and sellers to evaluate the credit worthiness of the buyer and quality of work of the seller.

9. **Transaction trail.** Buyers will require the capability to track purchases and shipments online. This means that buyers need to be able to access the seller's warehouse and factory to get an idea of when they can expect delivery of the product.

10. **Quality assurance.** Buyers, over time, will require the exchange to provide online evaluations of the participating vendors. The buyers want to know what other buyer experiences have been before entering into an agreement.

11. **Quality content.** Providing news and information about your industry is important. Having a section of the site for members of

the exchange to post press releases and offer industry studies is a good way to keep the attention of the exchange members.

12. **Credit availability.** Buyers need to be able to access credit for purchases through the exchange. The credit options need to range from online credit cards to loans to letters of credit provided electronically for foreign and domestic sales.

Examples of Success

There are a lot of well-financed companies in the B2B exchange space. In this chapter, I picked VerticalNet because their business model meets all twelve requirements for developing a successful B2B exchange. Right now, there are 2,600 B2B exchanges listed on Yahoo! as of fall of 2001. The reason B2B exchanges will grow and thrive is because buyers can find what they want and buy what they need at the best available price. In addition, the sellers can reduce their cost of doing business because the exchange is bringing them together with buyers who may never have heard of them.

Below is a chart that gives you insight into what it costs to build, maintain, and develop their Web sites into successful businesses.

VerticalNet

Initial cost to build Web site	$30 million
Cost to maintain Web site	$1 to $10 million
Full-time technologists/content developers	80 content, 160 technology
No. of salespeople	220
Employee time commitment	70 hours per week
Projected growth of sales department	50% next 3 years
Biggest day-to-day concern	Retaining people

VerticalNet

Marketing techniques	Trade shows
	Direct marketing
	Push e-mail
	Print advertising
Best marketing techniques	Print advertising
	Trade shows
Projected growth of marketing budget	300% to 500% next 3 years
Strategic partnerships	3-M, Microsoft

VerticalNet Interview

The following is an interview with Mark Welsh, president and CEO of VerticalNet, that delves into the cost and strategies his company is focused on to maintain its lead in developing B2B exchanges. Welsh is one of the best communicators in corporate America.

Prior to joining VerticalNet, Welsh was a senior vice president and corporate officer at America Online. He founded and ran AOL Enterprise, the B2B division of AOL. Prior to AOL, Welsh was the president of GEnie, the online service owned by GE. He also was the president of Information Kinetics, Inc., a venture capital–backed interactive information company focusing on the recruitment and classified advertising market. He graduated from Union College in 1976 with a BA in American studies, and Harvard Business School in 1980 with an MBA.

What type of financial commitment does it take to build a successful Web site?

To do it successfully, you need to get the audience, and that is done with engaging commerce. We believe good content equals good commerce.

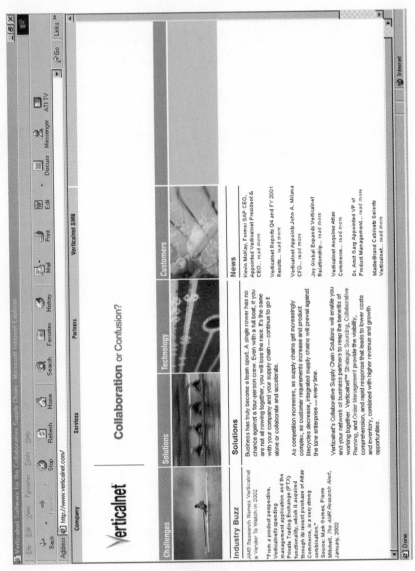

www.verticalnet.com

What are the three to five critical success factors by which you measure yourselves?

The first and most obvious is top-line revenue growth. The second is managing costs, although on the Internet that is hard to justify. The third metric is doing what we say we are going to do publicly. This is very important in the Internet market. The fourth is hiring all the best people to do what you say you are going to do. Fifth is don't believe your own hype. Stay focused, be smart, be moral, and have a good time. The Internet is so full of exaggeration, and we need to stay focused as a company.

What is your biggest day-to-day concern?

People! The Internet is one of the greatest land rushes of all time. There are so many temptations to leave for another company. Motivating them with opportunity and stock options is an ongoing challenge. As a footnote, it is easier in Philadelphia than in New York or San Francisco where headhunters are walking the hallways.

How important is first mover advantage in your coverage area?

I think it is pretty important. It has a cascading importance. The first value to it is with investors. We were lucky to be one of the early companies singing the B2B tune. This means we were able to control a lot of meeting agendas. We were able to give our vision. Everything we promised our private and public funders, we have delivered.

First mover is important in terms of establishing partnerships. Because we were known, people contacted us. Finally, we benefited greatly in terms of acquisitions or other investments. We get contacted about acquiring or investing in other companies.

What does your organization do to retain users?

We focus on three things:

1. We send them a welcome kit in paper and online. It describes how other companies have used us successfully in the past.
2. We have a password-protected part of the site called Virtual Office. It manages sales leads for our advertisers. It tells them what companies and individuals are using the site.
3. In the final months of the contract, the person who sold it contacts the user again and then goes over the success stories for the year.

What is the most difficult part of retaining users?

Sadly, one who didn't see the value from the beginning of the sale and therefore didn't use it during the year. Our renewal rates are extremely good. We will let users know what they aren't doing, such as using links, putting up new products, and keeping data updated.

What new technologies do you plan to deploy to make the user experience better that will result in more users?

We are going to have country-specific sites. We are going to have greater bidder experience. This will allow people to find new or used products, or those from a specific vendor. We will send reminders. They will have a large menu to choose from. We are creating customized versions for our users. You will be able to follow the industry and contact customers and associates when you need to. This is very similar to My Yahoo!.

What didn't you expect that turned out well?

Auction efforts will gain a lot more traffic than I would have thought.

What didn't you expect that didn't turn out well?

We expected that store fronts would grow a lot quicker and they haven't.

Chapter Summary

Building B2B exchanges may be the most lucrative model on the Internet. Over the next few years, all of the best real estate will be taken. To build an enduring business exchange, companies have to do the following:

1. **Recruit strong leadership that can communicate.** The people who run and promote the company to buyers have to have a large database of contacts. Credibility with the end user is critical. The CEO has to be able to sell his vision better than his competitors.

2. **Provide an easy-to-use site.** The users are busy people. They want to use an exchange that is as easy as driving their car. Each time a user has to make more than two or three clicks, the danger increases that the user will leave.

3. **Offer marquee participants**. Name brands have to be associated with the site in order to attract users.

4. **Attract visibility**. First mover advantage attracts visibility. Don't underestimate your marketing costs. Many of my clients believe if they hire a top-notch public relations firm and attract a lot of publicity, they won't have to spend as much on marketing. The reality is that public relations is a part of marketing, and to develop a successful campaign, you have to deliver your message on a consistent basis. This means having a public relations firm or someone internal aggressively soliciting print, online, radio, and television media; running and co-hosting seminars; setting up your top executives to speak at conferences, trade shows, and targeted user groups; and advertising, if you are attacking a large market.

   It has been my experience that whatever you think your budget is, multiply it by a factor of 2 to 10. The best way to figure out your marketing budget is to create a spreadsheet of every weapon you plan to use and multiply it by the number of people you plan to educate.

5. **Offer access to capital.** Partner up with a national bank to offer instant credit on large purchases. Have users of the site fill out credit applications as part of the sign-up process so they have access to capital if they need it.

6. **Raise a lot of capital.** Although we all expect big things from the B2B market, don't be surprised if results take longer than expected. Traditional business relationships and ways of doing business are hard to change. Make sure you have enough capital to stay the course.

7. **Understand that buyers and sellers win.** Any exchange where either side feels cheated or doesn't see value is doomed to failure. The exchanges that throw deals into cyberspace as if they are raw pieces of meat to be eaten by hungry lions will eventually run out of meat and be eaten by the lions.

Finally, the best technology is easy to acquire because it only costs money. To win in this space you have to either focus on building exchanges where there are few dominant players or plan to play in the space where there are dominant players such as the automotive industry. If you choose this route, you have to convince the behemoths that they are better owning a piece of you than taking the time, resources, and money building their own.

Chapter 12
Financial Services

IN CHAPTER 8, WE ADDRESSED FINANCIAL SERVICES as it relates to consumers. This chapter focuses on financial services from a B2B perspective. The two companies that are featured at the end of this chapter—Vcall, and Investorforce—receive all of their income from corporations, but many of their users tap into their Web sites from a home-based computer. This means that the design of the site has to be configured for the slowest modems, which at the time I am writing this book are 56K.

5 Types of Financial B2B Models

There is a variety of companies that provide financial services, marketplaces, and information to corporations. There are five major types of financial services/marketplaces you will find on the Internet that sell services to corporations:

1. *Banking.* Companies, like individuals, are paying their bills to corporations without any paper. The banks are working with companies like FreeMarkets, which provides companies with the ability to do e-commerce with their vendors and to pay bills online.

2. *Investment capital.* There are sites such as *www.vcapital.com* that provide companies access to individual, institutional, and corporate investors.

3. *Investor relations.* Vcall (*www.vcall.com*) provides publicly traded corporations with audio and text information for their individual and institutional shareholders.

4. *Investment banking.* There are sites like *www.witcapital.com* that provide companies with online access to individual investors in order to raise capital to grow their business.

5. *Money management.* InvestorForce.com (*www.investor force.com*) brings together plan sponsors, pension consultants, and money managers. Plan sponsors oversee each corporation's pension fund. Pension consultants interview money managers and recommend which money manager would be best to manage the plan sponsor's money. Money managers, according to the Federal Reserve, manage over a trillion dollars. The money comes from corporate, city, county, state, federal, and nonprofit pension funds and endowments. This is your 401K and traditional pension plans and donations made to foundations.

8 Elements for Building a Successful Financial Services Site

The companies that are successful in providing financial services to corporations focus on providing the following:

1. **Databases.** Members of financial services Web sites want access to databases that are constantly updated, that provide information on other members of the site, and that provide industry-marketing data. InvestorForce.com provides information on money managers and individual plan sponsors. The databases are updated daily.

2. **Interactivity.** Members want to participate in chat rooms with industry leaders and target clients to get insights into market needs. Companies such as InvestorForce allow buyers and sellers to exchange information about their specific needs without actually selling each other anything. Plan sponsors want to know the types of funds money managers are planning to create to provide better returns, and money managers want to know the types of funds in which specific plan sponsors are interested in investing. InvestorForce allows the interested parties to communicate through chat rooms and online surveys, which are sponsored by the money managers.

3. **Information.** Members want daily information feeds specific to their industry. They want to listen to what industry leaders have to say when they are saying it, or at least be able to download the discussion later in the day when their schedules are free. Most small public companies have a difficult time providing timely information to their individual stockholders. Maintaining a professional investor relations person(s) and providing information typically cost over $100,000 a year, according to the American Society of Investor Relations Professionals. Many companies outsource this work to investor relations firms.

4. **Online meetings.** Members are trying to hold down costs for running seminars for targeted customers and for supplying information to investors about the state of their companies. Vcall uses audio and video technology to allow public corporations to communicate with individual and institutional investors. InvestorForce.com uses the Internet for money managers to conduct meetings with multiple pension consultants and plan sponsors. These online meetings are a cross between a telephone conference and video conferencing, and they are economically feasible.

5. **E-mail.** Members are being alerted daily about new information that can be found on the Web site, which helps drive traffic on a daily basis.

6. **Customization.** Companies that bank online, pay bills online, and use online services to manage their employees' retirement accounts demand customization. They want to go to a site that provides them with information that is most relevant to their business. For example, a company that uses multiple money managers to manage its company's 401K accounts wants its 401K internal home page to show each mutual fund being offered to employees, their returns to date, comparisons between the other funds offered to employees, and online application and withdrawal forms for employees.

7. **Calendars.** Companies and individuals want to use online calendars to remind them about important events related to the financial service company they are using. For example, individuals who sign up with Investorbroadcast are interested in being reminded about conference calls for specific stocks that they own. Individuals can enter into their online calendar which stocks they own, and Investorbroadcast will automatically update their personal calendars based on their equity holdings.

8. **E-mail newsletters.** E-mail newsletters are more cost and user effective than traditional newsletters. Many of us who get traditional newsletters tend to stack them up in a pile because we have given e-mail priority over traditional mail, unless, of course, we are looking for a check. E-mail newsletters also tend to have a wider readership because they are easier to distribute.

Examples of Success

The financial field has been using the Internet to change its business models to make them more efficient and profitable and to attract and retain customers. Online brokerage firms such as E*Trade are now consistently profitable, and online banks are not far behind. If you follow the stock market and buy your own stocks, why wouldn't you want to buy them online? If you have children in college, wouldn't it be convenient to communicate regularly with them online about their courses, social lives, and, of course, their mounting credit card bills?

The examples in this chapter are companies that have used the Internet to build a business that is changing the way traditional businesses in their field operate.

Our first example is InvestorForce.com, which provides pension funds with a more efficient way to find money management firms to manage their money. Until InvestorForce.com was born, pension consultants used databases to find which money managers had the best performance records, and then recommended to their clients which money managers they should interview. InvestorForce.com is reducing the time and cost for pension fund managers and pension consultants to find the right managers to manage their money.

The second example is Investorbroadcast. Before the advent of the Internet, anyone who invested in publicly traded companies could find out information about their companies only through quarterly mailings; annual reports; by attending a shareholders meeting, if the company was holding it within driving distance; or through the newspaper. Today companies outsource their investor relations to Investorbroadcast so that it can provide company information quickly and efficiently to their stockholders. Stockholders can now listen to conference calls and watch stockholder meetings without leaving their homes.

Below is a chart that shows what each company has done to build and maintain its Web site and competitive position.

	InvestorForce.com	Investorbroadcast
Initial cost to build Web site	$500,000	$1 million
Cost to maintain Web site	$5–$10 million	$500,000 plus
Full-time technologists/ content developers	35	45
No. of salespeople	15	10
Projected growth of sales department	25	30–40
Employee time commitment	50–60 hours per week	50–60 hours per week
Biggest day-to-day concern	Retaining traffic/ building barriers	Retaining employees Raising competitive barriers Attracting capital
Marketing techniques	Public relations Direct mail Opt-in e-mail Print advertising Seminars	Public relations Opt-in e-mail Online newsletter Online calendar Affiliates program
Best marketing techniques	Targeted e-mail	Affiliates program E-mail
Projected growth of marketing budget	300% plus	
Strategic partnerships	None	None

InvestorForce.com Interview

Colin Wahl is founder/CMO of InvestorForce.com. Prior to starting InvestorForce.com, Wahl was president/COO of Dakin & Willison, a financial services marketing firm focused on working with money managers. Before becoming president of Dakin & Willison, Wahl was a vice president at SEI Investments and was in charge of marketing and branding their money management business. He has a BS in

www.investorforce.com

accounting from the University of Toronto and an MBA from the University of Michigan.

What type of financial commitment does it take to build a successful Web site?

Our first site cost less than $500,000, but that was really more of a demo than a site we could use to sell our customers. To do it right will vary from community to community. If you are trying to build an in-depth community like we are, you are talking a minimum of $10 to $15 million. That entails building an organization structure to support the Web site. You need to have a good internal technical organization. Without that, you don't have a product.

You need someone to build audience development. You need a product development group to come up with new ideas. You need salespeople to call on salespeople and client service people to support your members. An operations group has to be in place to make sure license agreements and partnerships are put in place. It can't be fly by night. You need a lot of capital for potential acquisitions.

What are the three to five critical success factors by which you measure yourselves?

We measure ourselves through traffic, how often they come back, and how many people sign on and pay to be a part of our community. It boils down to one thing—who have we been able to attract and make come back to the site? It's making sure you get the target audience you are going after. Most sites are like ours in that the users have to register, and the vast majority are our target audience and the others are irrelevant.

How important is first mover advantage?

First mover advantage is critical. This whole business is a learning game. You are going to make mistakes and you will learn from them, and competitors who follow you are going to make some of the same mistakes, but you are a step ahead of them. You will know before they do what is lurking around the corner.

What does your organization do to retain users?

We basically try to give them a satisfying and rewarding experience. We e-mail them when new things are added. We have an advisory board of our users. They give us feedback into new enhancements and features and review them prior to our putting them on the Web site.

What is the most difficult part of retaining users?

I think it is helping them achieve and meet the needs that they have. In our case it is providing them with something that will make their job easier. If we accomplish this, then they will come back.

What is unique about your site that makes users want to bookmark it?

There are a number of things. There is a lot they can get from our site that they can't get elsewhere. One is an investment manager performance database. We have various tools that allow users to share insights and information. We do this through surveys, product analysis, and setting up conferences.

What new technologies do you plan to deploy to make the user experience better that will result in more users?

One that we plan to use is embedded e-mail function. We basically set up a communication center in our Web site that gives our users the ability to interact with their suppliers and consultants.

We plan to enhance their ability to execute RFPs online. When it makes sense, we will integrate video technology at some level.

What didn't you expect that turned out well?

I was pleasantly surprised at the interest in the community. I didn't think we would attract them as quickly as we have.

What didn't you expect that didn't turn out well?

I didn't expect it to be so difficult to retain them. We have had to make a much larger investment in marketing.

Vcall Interview

David Bauman is the president and CEO of Vcall, the leading broadcaster of investor events over the Internet. Prior to joining Vcall, Bauman served as senior vice president of the Interactive Services Group at American Express. He formed the Interactive Group at Amex in 1994, after identifying online services as critical to the company's future. While at Amex, Bauman and his organization introduced many products and services to the market, including ExpressNet, Amex's award-winning service on both America Online and the Web. Under his leadership, the Interactive Group introduced services linking Amex cardmembers to Intuit's Quicken and Microsoft's Money software. Before forming the Interactive Services Group, Bauman was vice president of Strategic Planning at American Express, where he led reengineering efforts and developed new telecommunications business for the company. From 1985 to 1992, Bauman was with the international strategy consulting firm of Bain & Company, which is based in San Francisco. Bauman received a BS in chemistry and an MS in engineering-economic systems from Stanford University. He received his MBA with High Distinction from the Harvard Business School.

What size of financial commitment should a company be thinking of to maintain its site?

If you are building a scalable site you probably can't build it for less than $1 million, and you are going to spend hundreds of thousands

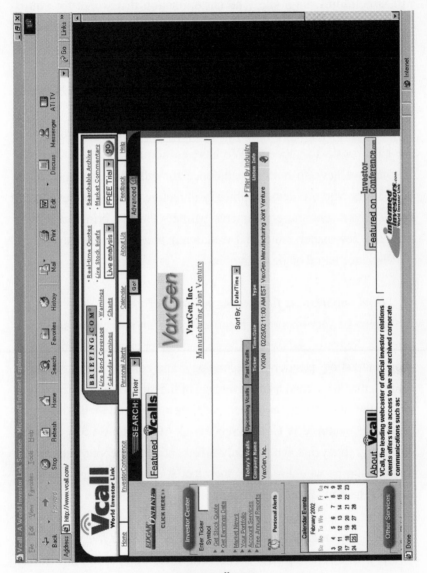

www.vcall.com

of dollars a year to maintain it. You are talking about databases and the infrastructure to run a site. The customization that works for you is quite costly. The front end with an appropriate look and feel needs to be constantly updated or it can look old.

What are the three to five critical success factors by which you measure yourselves?

We are a media company. Our business is straightforward in what we have to do to succeed. We have to acquire relevant content. Second, we have to build an audience for our content and develop loyal users who are demographically attractive. Third, we have to go out to advertisers and e-commerce partners that we bring value. We are like a newspaper, radio, or TV station in that we can give a value to our audience based on demographics.

How important is first mover advantage?

It can be very important. It carries risks with it. It can be an advantage or a double-edged sword. The second mover can learn from the first about marketing, positioning, technology, and content. Sometimes it is the case that the second takes advantage of the mistakes of the first.

If the first mover can't keep pace, then they lose their advantage. A perfect example is CompuServe and AOL. Steve Case of AOL would say five years ago that only 3 percent of the people were on the Internet and he would focus on the other 97 percent, which he did so well that he now owns CompuServe.

Will your marketing budget go up over the next five years?

It will only go up. Our model will never be to spend millions to build brand. In our world the best marketing we can do is to have the best content around. We want investors to look at us as one of the best sources of investor information. We are focused on insight, because news is a commodity. We want to help investors become successful.

What does your organization do to retain users?

The two most important things we do are:

1. We deliver high quality content. This company was founded on the premise that individual and professional investors can make use of information that was available to only a few people on Wall Street and some money managers. We have opened it up to the entire investing public. We are committed to giving them insight and access to the inner circle.

2. Some still don't come back. With that said, we use our newsletter and our e-mail alert system to get them to come back.

What is the most difficult part of retaining users?

The most difficult part is remaining relevant. We are like a broadcast outlet. We have archives, but every day we need to be relevant.

What types of technical and nontechnical skills are you looking for now?

Among our needs now are streaming video and overall media. We have outsourced our development to the Sycamore Group. We will need business development and salespeople with Web experience. They are worth their weight in gold. We need financial journalists.

What is unique about your site that makes users want to bookmark it?

Our content is unique, period. It is the kind of content that gives you insights on companies, CEOs, and Wall Street, and the way we use streaming media gives serious investors a lot of value.

What new technologies do you plan to deploy to make the user experience better that will result in more users?

The big question is when does video become a more significant part of our business. Most of our users hear video and see charts. When the cost of video comes down, and when the user has a faster modem, and when getting people on video is as easy as audio, then video will become more useful and then that transition will occur.

What didn't you expect that turned out well?

There are two things that advertisers want and that is to be memorable and to be seen in a positive light. Traditionally, advertising didn't deliver instant transactions—until the Web. The only problem is that banner click-through rates are .05 percent and dropping. We have begun to pioneer to put together audio and video to transact business on the Web.

As an example, because we develop half our own material, we can have our commentator tell something about our sponsor and have the listener click immediately to that sponsor's link. We are in the very early stages. We have seen one to two orders of magnitude of growth by using this over the standard banner. We think this is a tremendous benefit for the sponsor.

What didn't you expect that didn't turn out well?

We are disappointed as both a buyer and seller of advertising. Advertising is still fragmented. There are few integrated advertising agencies. There are few that think of fully integrated cross-media advertising campaigns. We expected to be there by now, but we aren't.

What is the future of destination sites on the Internet?

I think paper is great and I read lots of books. I don't think the Web can replace all of that. I think people have an unlimited need for information. If we look out five or ten years into the future, all timely and archival information will be found on or through the Web. It might replace the daily newspaper, but not books. The ability of the computer and the Web is to find information for me and tell me what I ought to know and do.

Chapter Summary

Right now the financial services field is primarily focused on banking, investor relations, and money management related services. The ability to buy business-related insurance will come soon. To develop a solid business model in financial services, you need to do well in three areas:

1. **Industry focus.** Focus on financial segments that have either high volume, such as providing insurance or loans, or high margins, such as marketing money management services to corporations and wealthy individuals. In the commercial insurance environment, corporations are looking to reduce everything from health care to business insurance to officers and directors liability insurance.

2. **Community.** Focus on attracting only the users who value the information your target customer will pay for. For companies like E*Trade, the market for users is in the millions. Companies that have a defined audience with a defined need include Vcall, which focuses strictly on providing a service for public companies, and InvestorForce.com, which focuses on providing information to money managers, plan sponsors, and pension consultants.

3. **Technology.** Focus on using technology such as chat rooms that brings together people to share ideas without having to travel. Or use technology as a way to reduce the cost of disseminating news and information to large numbers of people, which is a major problem for publicly traded companies.

Chapter 13
Business Services/Products

THERE IS A TREMENDOUS AMOUNT OF OPPORTUNITY in offering business products and services over the Internet. As I write this book, publicly traded Internet companies are taking a beating, but research shows that businesses are more excited about the prospects of the Internet today than they were two years ago.

Approximately one-third of small businesses in the United States are now online, according to a recent study commissioned by Prodigy Biz Corp., a subsidiary of Prodigy Communications Corporation. Additionally, 40 percent of small businesses without Web sites (approximately 2.1 million) expect to be on the Internet within an average of the next eight months.

The study, which was carried out by International Communications Research, found that 90 percent of small businesses in the United States anticipate benefiting from the Internet. However, 66 percent do not believe that the Web offers significant growth opportunities because they are local businesses.

Primary uses of the Internet cited by respondents were: promoting to prospects (69 percent), e-commerce (57 percent), providing better customer service (48 percent), competing with other businesses (46 percent), and communicating with employees (11 percent).

Among those surveyed, 25 percent of companies with fewer than ten employees have an Internet presence, versus 50 percent of those with ten or more employees. Over 40 percent of small business owners claim that they do not have the staff or the time to maintain a Web site. However, nearly 75 percent say that cost is not a barrier.

Office supplies is an approximately $1.3 billion business and is expected to climb to $65 billion by 2003 (Forrester Research). The two biggest categories in terms of usage by businesses of all sizes are not Internet or information systems. They are business supplies and printing services, according to the Small Business Administration. As you can see, the amount of potential sales is tremendous for the providers of products and services for businesses.

Word	No. of Categories	No. of Sites
Business supplies	204	20,145
Printing	6	3,663

I have my own small business, and I help other small businesses get launched. Practically every business service and product you need can be bought without speaking to anyone and without worrying whether the seller is open for business. Here are examples of business services that can be bought on the Internet and companies that supply them.

Service	Web site
Incorporation	Access.com
Domain registration	Register.com
Stationery	iPrint.com
Web site development	Homestead.com
Office supplies	Staples.com
Corporate credit card	Americanexpress.com
Online banking	TheBancorp.com

Service	Web site (continued)
Bank loan	sbasmallbusinessloans.com
Tax preparation	Intuit.com
Business insurance	Quotesmith.com
Health insurance	Ehealth.com
Computer technology support	Askdrtech.com
Marketing service	Smarterworks.com
Sales lead generation	RFPmarket.com
Accounting	Accounting.com
Legal	USLaw.com
Business plans	Bplans.com
Public relations	PR Newswire
Hotel	Hotels.com
Air travel	Rosenbluth.com
Car rental	Avis.com
Train	Amtrak.com
Software discounts	Microsoft.com
Industry magazines	Tradepub.com
Utility (telephone/electric discounts)	Omnichoice
Entertainment	Tickets.com
Research sites	CyberAtlas.com

10 Elements to Developing a Successful Business Products/Services Web Site

The competition is so great for selling business products and services that owners of such sites have to create opportunities for buyers to find what they need at prices below or the same as they would find in stores, and to offer opportunities to make money while they are shopping.

1. **Delivery speed.** Anyone who goes to *www.officedepot.com* doesn't want to hear that an order takes three days to deliver. If

buyers can't get what they want within a day, then the service becomes irrelevant.

2. **Interactivity.** The ability to actually create and approve your stationery, business cards, brochures, and other printing needs online makes a site such as *www.iprint.com,* which is featured in this chapter, very special and a great use of Internet technology.

3. **Pricing.** The ability to buy at prices below what you would pay in the store or at a printer is paramount to attracting and retaining users. This writer went to iPrint.com to design and buy stationery. The stationery cost 25 percent less than local printers wanted to charge and was delivered in less time than local printers could do it.

4. **Product offering.** Every product that can be found in a store or a store's catalog has to be available on the company's Web site or the Web loses value.

5. **Product availability.** No buyer should have to go through the experience of loading up their online shopping cart only to find 25 percent of what they need or the one or two most important items they selected are out of stock. The major national office supply companies know how much stock to carry from their catalog sales experience.

6. **Shipment tracking.** Although buyers expect to get their supplies overnight, in the event products don't arrive the next day, buyers want to know that they can track their shipments to see when they might arrive or if the orders were never fulfilled.

7. **Sales leads.** This element will seem unusual to most readers, but companies like *www.officedepot.com*, which is spotlighted in this chapter, realize that buyers don't just want to purchase products at a business site, they want to be a part of an online business community. That means that merchants aren't just buying from other merchants, they are receiving opportunities to sell their own goods and services. OfficeDepot.com is one of the first online business supply stores to provide that service and create that atmosphere of

a real e-commerce community. They realized that although their brand name is well known, so is their competition, and they recognized the need to provide another reason for business owners to come and buy from their Web site. OfficeDepot.com developed alliances with a variety of business service providers in the areas of insurance, legal, and money management in order to attract and maintain customers. By providing access to these services, Office Depot created an online community for small business owners and those serving them.

8. **Search engine.** Buyers don't want to have to spend a lot of time clicking through a site to find what they want. They require that the site have a search engine that allows them to name the product or service or the provider of the product to find the service that they want.

9. **News.** The sites that provide business news and insights give users another reason to bookmark those sites. For regional business suppliers, they can help provide local business news by giving free space on their sites for customers to post press releases.

10. **Free products.** Buyers will come back to sites that provide links to free products such as software.

Examples of Success

When I researched the business services and product space, I was amazed at how much revenue traditional and Internet-only companies were generating by selling their products and services over the Internet. Dell Computer over the last three years went from selling a few hundred million dollars' worth of computers over the Internet to almost $10 billion over the Internet. When I interviewed officials at Office Depot, they said that if their Internet business were a stand-alone company, they would still be profitable.

For this chapter, I picked one company, iPrint.com, that is changing one of the oldest and most established industries, printing, from a business where individual customers physically go to a printer, select stationery and other paper items by looking in books, and see a mock up of their information, to a business where customers create their stationery and other products directly on the Internet.

The second example is OfficeDepot.com, which uses the Internet as a way to provide greater convenience and reduce cost for attracting and supporting customers. The cost for Office Depot to sell their products over the Internet is minimal because their distribution facilities and product databases already exist.

Below is a chart that shows what size investment it took to get the business off the ground, developed, and promoted.

Companies	iPrint.com	Office Depot
Initial cost to build Web site	$500,000 plus	$1 million
Cost to maintain Web site	$1 million plus	$1 million
Full-time technologists/ content developers	75	30
No. of salespeople	15	None
Projected growth of sales department	20%	None
Employee time commitment	50–60 hours per week	40–50 hours per week
Biggest day-to-day concern	Order processing	Scale up and integrate older systems

Companies	iPrint.com	Office Depot
Marketing techniques	Direct mail Partnerships Public relations	Print Direct mail E-mail Banner advertisements Partnerships
Best marketing techniques	Direct mail Partnerships	E-mail Banners Direct mail
Projected growth of marketing budget	2–3 times	25%
Strategic partnerships	None	E-letter Telepost E-stamp Scheduleonline

iPrint.com Interview

Royal Farros is the president of iPrint.com. Before founding iPrint.com in 1996, Farros, forty, was cofounder and chairman of the board of T/Maker Company, a Silicon Valley software company named three consecutive years to *Inc.* magazine's List of the Top 500 Fastest Growing Privately Held Companies in America. Twice named as one of America's top 100 entrepreneurs aged thirty or under by the Association of Collegiate Entrepreneurs, Farros has also been included in the prestigious *MicroTimes* 100 List of Industry Leaders. Farros has authored articles in leading industry journals, including *MicroTimes*. Farros received his BS and MS degrees in industrial engineering from Stanford University (1981 and 1983 respectively).

www.iprint.com

What do you need to provide users to make a successful community site?

I am a big believer in giving consumers deals that they can't refuse. You need to make your offers really compelling. You have to think about what will make them come back daily. What are we offering that they can't refuse? It has to be incredibly useful. Our mission is to create things people want to buy.

How do you find out what your potential users want out of an online community?

One of my golden rules is to be your own best customer. I am not saying I know what all my customers want, but because I am a customer, I believe I know what I would want. I want to create stationery and promotional items without the hassle of driving back and forth to a local print shop. I want to put pictures on mouse pads and mugs and create personalized golf balls as fun gifts for my friends who play golf. Finally, I don't want to pay an arm and a leg.

We read every single comment our customers send to us. This way, we can refine what our customers want and find new business opportunities.

What size of financial commitment should a company be thinking of to maintain its site?

It depends on what you are doing. Although we use technology to keep our costs low, we still have a people-intensive operation. We currently employ over 160 people, and we also private-label our site for other major companies. If our partners grow, then we will add more people.

With custom printing of just business cards, there are a lot of issues involved, such as ink colors, paper type, whether the inks are falling off the side or are raised, and so on. Typically, you'd need to work with your printer on all of these decisions.

We believe that iPrint.com is the most complex e-commerce site on the Internet. Selling books and CDs only requires having a database that contains the names of specific books and CDs. Customization doesn't enter into the picture. That is why it is hard to say how much it costs to maintain and improve a complex site like ours as opposed to a site that doesn't require customizing the products.

What are the three to five critical success factors by which you measure yourselves?

1. *Reprint-due-to-error rate.* If you ask us to make something, we build it and try to meet your expectations. If it doesn't look a certain way, then you are unhappy. If you are unhappy, you are going to return it and we are going to reprint it. The cause could have been a technical problem or one of our printers having a bad day. That is a quantitative way for us to track how happy our customers are, and we track it religiously. The lower that number, the better job we are doing. Our reprint-due-to-error rate is about 1 to 2 percent, which compares to 15 percent for traditional print shops.

   When you walk into a print shop, you have to look through business card stylebooks, choose fonts and your layout, and guess how it will look when it's printed. At iPrint.com, consumers can design their cards right on our site, and that is why we are 10 to 15 times more reliable than typical bricks-and-mortar print shops. By giving consumers the opportunity to design and proof their work, we offer a definite advantage over traditional print shops. When we send a job to the printer, the customer has already seen and approved the design and layout.

2. *Number of visitors.* This tells us how successful we are in attracting people to our site.

3. *Sell-through rate.* This indicates that we are being successful in getting people to design and order from iPrint.com.

Do you have an affiliates program, and how has it worked?

You sign up and we put a link on your site and then have it tagged. We will pay you an affiliate commission of 2 to 10 percent.

Have you developed strategic partnerships and have they brought in new business?

Yes! We have thousands of partners and they are divided into the following categories:

*   Affiliate labels—we have thousands of these partners.
*   Colabels—we have hundreds of these partners.
*   Private labels—we have a handful of these partners.

What does your organization do to retain users?

We have a customer loyalty program. We go to our customers with special promotions all the time. We've developed a "five-second special," which features a picture of the item, a short description, and discount amount. We do this two to three times a month. Customers should be able to decide on this purchase quickly and not waste a lot of their time.

What is the most difficult part of retaining users?

Because we are in the printing industry, it is all about product quality. The printing must be on time and process must be top rate so our end product is top rate.

What new technologies do you plan to deploy to make the user experience better that will result in more users?

It's a tough question. We need to make the site faster, which makes it more useful. We are using more 3-D technology, which you can see at the Intel Outfitters site. It allows consumers to design a coffee mug, rotate it, and see how the design looks in 3-D before ordering.

What didn't you expect that turned out well?

Something we are living through right now. We are the most heavily used print portal. What we didn't expect was the range of orders we had to cover. Most of the orders that people have been placing are $60 to $70, but today we are getting requests from people who have print jobs that run into the thousands of dollars. This has caused us to offer a broader array of services.

What didn't you expect that didn't turn out well?

I thought our concept was going to be brilliant. I thought the whole way banners were being done was wrong. People were making them graphically beautiful. I thought if we made it simple and straightforward and said "Don't click here unless you are looking for inexpensive business cards," that it would drive people to our site. We found that this didn't produce any better results.

What is the future of your industry on the Internet?

I think it will be very big. I think every print shop will eventually be online. We are also the largest provider of online technology for the print industry, so we hope the online printing industry as a whole continues to grow.

Office Depot.com Interview

Keith Butler is OfficeDepot.com's vice president, acting in the capacity as general manager of the OfficeDepot.com organization. Butler brings extensive interactive and marketing experience to Office Depot Online. Prior to Office Depot, he served as vice president, Business Development for Preview Travel, one of the most popular commerce sites on the Web. Butler joined Preview Travel from GNN/America Online, as vice president, Online Sales. Butler graduated from California State University at Chico with a BS in political science.

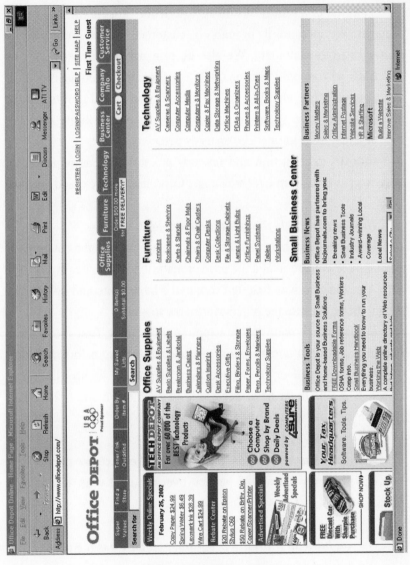

www.officedepot.com

What are the three to five critical success factors by which you measure yourselves?

The first criterion is customer experience. That is the true measurement. We measure it through our customer service group and by messages from customers. We also do primarily online surveys. We also track what people visit on our site on an aggregated basis.

Second is revenue. We look at gross revenues and profits and we are profitable as a stand-alone business. I want to know how the industry analysts and financial analysts perceive us.

Industry recognition and rewards are the last component. We have won awards from *CIO* magazine, Information Week, and Yahoo!

How important is first mover advantage?

It is important, but it isn't decisive. It depends on the category of e-commerce you are in and the pace of maturity of the category.

Amazon.com was first and captured a huge share and no one has caught them, because the others were slow to react.

On the other hand, look at pet supplies. The first mover was PetSmart and in a short period of time there were a lot of quality players that joined in. The same thing happened with online drug stores. None of them have been able to grab the market share that Amazon.com did with books.

Will your marketing budget go up over the next five years?

It will go up at least 25 percent over the next year. It's hard to predict out past that.

Do you have an affiliates program, and how has it worked?

We are just starting to initiate one. That is something that needs to be managed very carefully. First of all, any type of affiliates program requires a revenue sharing model. Margins are very small and so you have to pay careful attention to that.

What does your organization do to retain users?

We have a number of features on the site. We have custom shopping lists and special order forms. We provide content and editorial that is interesting to the customer. We call it transactive content. It talks about how to get organized and provides insights into how to improve business. We link that editorial to products that might help users improve that aspect of their business.

What is the most difficult part of retaining users?

We aren't trend or fashion based. We are need-based products. It's the fulfillment and customer service element. It's making sure what you order arrives on time. We put it on our own truck and drop it off wherever it is supposed to be delivered.

What is unique about your site that makes users want to bookmark it?

It is a fully integrated e-commerce site. You can see whether the item you want to purchase is available. Second, we deliver ourselves so it is tied up into the system. The fulfillment part has been the biggest bugaboo for e-commerce companies and we have conquered that.

What new technologies do you plan to deploy to make the user experience better that will result in more users?

We will do some personalization. We will add some content management. We will do some merchandizing management tools, again using personalization.

What didn't you expect that turned out well?

The value of the brand proved to be more valuable online.

What didn't you expect that didn't turn out well?

The pace of the ability to effect change on the Web site.

What is the future of your industry on the Internet?

We are in the toddler stage. This industry has huge potential. The growth of small business on the Internet has been rapid.

Chapter Summary

When you boil it down, a business supplier and printer has to offer the following six things:

1. More products than can be found in a bricks-and-mortar store.
2. The ability to take back products to a bricks-and-mortar store or have a delivery truck pick them up.
3. Products at a price below what buyers can get them for by going to a local merchant.
4. The ability to create one's own products without using a specialist.
5. Fast delivery.
6. Opportunities to interact and do business with other buyers.

Chapter 14
Government Commerce

THE AMOUNT OF MONEY SPENT BY local, county, state, and federal government agencies, non profit agencies and the private sector on products, services, and information related to the government is in the hundreds of billions of dollars, according to information supplied by the U.S. Census Bureau. The opportunities to sell products, services, and information are enormous because of the large number of local, state, and federal government agencies, and agencies within those agencies, as well as, private and non-profit sector individuals and organizations,buying products, and information from government agencies.

There are at least thirteen types of online government communities that can be created to service billion dollar marketplaces, and those opportunities are as follows:

1. Securities
2. Agricultural
3. Highways
4. Judicial
5. Law enforcement

6. Legislative
7. Military
8. Real estate
9. State-run universities
10. Science and research
11. School districts
12. Tax authorities
13. Transportation

What makes the government market for selling products, services, and obtaining information attractive is its enormous size and growth potential, especially in the aftermath of the terrorist attacks on the World Trade Center and the Pentagon, and the collapse of corporate giants such as Enron. Companies that focus on reducing the government's cost of doing business, helping the government sell excess inventory, and delivering information, have tremendous opportunities.

This chapter focuses on one opportunity and that is giving access to federally mandated information on companies that want to sell securities (paper that allows individuals or corporations to own shares in an incorporated company that must follow the rules set forth by federal and state governments) to the public or have sold securities to the public.

10 Elements to Building a Successful Government Content and E-commerce Web Site

Most people equate the word "government" with bureaucracy and confusion. The Internet has become a valuable tool in making government more accessible to the average person and at the same time helping government to lower the costs of providing services and collecting fees.

There are a variety of government oriented Web sites ranging from sites that allow government employees at the local, state, and federal level to procure products and services, all the way to publishing and selling government related information. In this chapter, we use EdgarOnline (*www.edgar-online.com*), which provides business securities related information that public companies are mandated to report to the Securities and Exchange Commission.

1. **Calendar.** Users want to know when government contracts are coming up for bid, when they have too file various taxes, and when different government reports are coming available.

2. **Education.** Users who have never bought excess government property or participated in a government auction will use sites that provide easy-to-understand, step-by-step directions on how to buy government surplus goods and property. A good example of this is *www.bestauctions.net*.

3. **Database.** Local, state, and private sector attorneys, money managers, individual investors, and non profit watch dog entities use EdgarOnline (*www.edgar-online.com*) to track quarterly and annual financial reports and disclosures of public companies. The reports are important to securities law enforcement officials to make sure public companies headquartered or doing business in their state are not breaking securities laws. Anyone who has followed Enron Corporation's fall realizes the value of this information for both the public and the government as they try to sort out the truths, lies, and responsibilities for tens of thousands of employees and investors losing all or part of their retirement capital.

4. **Directory.** Users that provide products and services to governments greatly value sites that provide a directory of contacts. Directories that aren't maintained on a regular basis cause the rest of the site to lose credibility.

5. **Financing.** Vendors who receive sizable government contracts want the ability to apply for lines of credit online.

6. **Interactivity.** Users who have grown accustomed to purchasing airline tickets, books, and stocks online, are now beginning to pay their

taxes online as well. The ability to access and download government related information is imperative.

7. **News.** Users want access to news bulletins and updates on specific government agencies they are marketing to. The types of information they are looking for are changes in the procurement process and changes in government management.

8. **Opportunities.** Users want to go to a site that provides them with procurement opportunities by type of government entity. Users also want to know which contractors won various contracts because they may be looking for partners to fulfill those contracts.

9. **Ratings.** Government procurement officers will be interested in using Web sites that provide ratings on vendors' ability to provide quality products and services. I could not find such a site at the time of writing this book, but many of the sites we contacted in the government arena are working on providing such a value-added service.

10. **Strategy.** Vendors who want to provide products and services to government agencies put a high value on Web sites that provide insights and strategies on how to best position themselves to obtain contracts.

Example of Success

Government agencies and for profit corporations are using the Internet to buy, sell, and provide products, services, and information. As we mentioned earlier in this chapter, individuals and corporations are becoming very adapt at buying online. The cost and reach of the Internet is greater than any other form of communication that has ever been created.

I selected EdgarOnline as the example for this chapter. EdgarOnline was launched in 1995 and went public in 1999. It was one of the first pure Internet companies to go public and to become profitable. Every investment house, broker, corporate attorney dealing with securities, corporate investor relations officer, business writer, and state securities agency uses EdgarOnline to get information about companies looking to offer shares in their company to the public or to track information about existing public companies.

Below is a chart that shows the size and scope of the investment made by EdgarOnline related to development of their site and core technologies and the type of personnel infrastructure, personnel commitment, and marketing tactics it takes to be a leader in a space.

Susan Strausberg, founder of EdgarOnline, has served as a member of the Board of Directors, CEO, and secretary since EdgarOnline was formed in November 1995. From December 1994 until the formation of EdgarOnline, Mrs. Strausberg was a consultant to Internet Financial Network. Mrs. Strausberg served on the Board of Directors of RKO Pictures from December 1998 to May 2001. Mrs. Strausberg, the wife of EdgarOnline's chairman, holds a B.A. degree from Sarah Lawrence College.

Edgar-Online

Initial cost to build Web site	$1 million plus
Cost to maintain Web site	$1 million plus
Full-time technologists/content developers	100
No. of salespeople	15
Projected growth of sales department	Public Company can't project
Employee time commitment	50-60 hours per week
Biggest day-to-day concern	Retaining clients
Marketing techniques	Public Relations Direct mail Push e-mail Print advertising
Best marketing techniques	Push e-mail

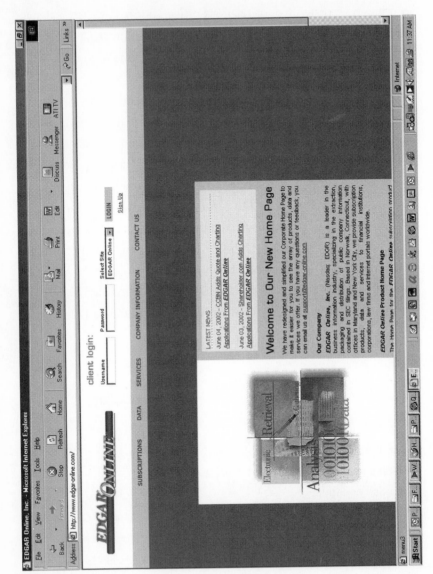

www.edgar-online.com

Edgar-Online (continued)

Projected growth of marketing budget	Public Company won't project future.
Strategic partnerships	Yahoo!, Lycos, Excite

What do you need to provide users to make a successful community site?

I don't think we would call what we offer an online community. We offer access to information and our business couldn't exist if there wasn't the Internet, but we aren't a community. To develop a destination that people will bookmark, you need to provide them with information they need or want. In our case, professionals and even individuals come to our site because we have information that they want in order to make a variety of financial decisions or to find out more about a public company.

How do you find out what your potential users want out of an online community?

In our case we have customer service representatives and salespeople who speak to our customers all the time.

What type of financial commitment does it take to build a successful Web site?

It takes millions of dollars to build a real time information service. The millions are in the technology. The cost is in developing the products that allow us to deliver the information that is useful for our clients. The cost of distribution is a minor, but critical, part of that.

What size of financial commitment should a company be thinking of to maintain their site?

It depends on what you are trying to accomplish, what you are offering, the size of your audience and if it's individuals or corporations that are using your service. If your primary market is the corporate market and you are housing lots of information on databases that needs to be accessed at anytime you are talking about significant costs.

Not only do you need money for technology, but for individuals to respond to phone and e-mail questions as they come in. Higher priced offerings targeted to the corporate and institutional market require a sales force to call on corporate clients to sell them your services and train them on using your service to benefit from it.

How many people do you have full-time working on the technical and non-technical side of the site?

We have 100 employees, of whom 60 are on the technical side and 40 are on the marketing, support, and administrative side.

What are the three to five critical success factors by which you measure yourselves?

1. Shareholder value
2. We focus on using the Web to bring users to our service offerings. We do this through relations with our partners, such as Yahoo!, that integrate EDGAR Online into their portals.
3. Getting our direct sales force into corporations and institutions.
4. Our service has to be mission critical, high service, industrial strength. We need to always be 100 percent robust, accurate, and fast.
5. Because we use machines and not people to provide our content, we have a high level of revenue per employee. The current ratio is $200,000 per employee.

What is your biggest day-to-day concern?

In the early days I used to lose sleep about the factors beyond our control such as the infrastructure of the Internet. Those types of problems have gone away. Now the issues that concern me are scalability and shareholder value.

How important is first mover advantage?

It's critical. If you get there first and execute your vision well, you create an enormous barrier to entry. If you do a sloppy job, you are the guy with the arrows in your back. If you do it right, you can build an impenetrable lead and control market share.

What marketing techniques are you using to drive traffic?

We start with strategic partnerships. We provide small amounts of our content to our partners such as Yahoo!, Lycos, AOL, and more than 200 financial sites who attract a broad audience of users of financial information. This familiarizes new prospects with our brand and makes them aware of our premium services. We database our users and use direct marketing to deliver our value message.

Which ones have worked the best?

The initial traffic drivers through our partners have worked the best. Our selling skills once users get to us are the second piece of that puzzle.

Do you have an affiliates program, and how has it worked?
No!

What does your organization do to retain users?

We focus on making and keeping our service the best. We survey our professional users and make sure they are happy with the information they are buying and try to learn what other content would be useful to them. We also have a six-person customer support group that is devoted to keeping our customers happy.

What is the most difficult part of retaining users?

Eighty percent of our revenue comes from corporate users and we have practically no turnover with this customer group. Individual users have a higher turnover rate for a variety of reasons. When we do exit interviews, we usually find that they may have subscribed in order to get one specific piece of information and since they are not repeat users they do not renew their subscriptions.

What didn't you expect that turned out well?

Since we were early Internet content providers, we did not anticipate the potential revenues that could be realized from advertising. As Internet advertising became a reality we were able to benefit from it. Now that it has declined we are sorry to see the dividend dwindle, but fortunately our overall strategy had no dependence on revenue from advertising. Although it was a primary goal to become the top brand worldwide for our information, I am still surprised by how quickly we have succeeded in reaching that goal.

What didn't you expect that didn't turn out well?
Nothing!

What is the future of your industry on the Internet?

We firmly believe that ultimately all financial information will be delivered and utilized on the Internet and that we will continue to grow market share in our industry.

Chapter Summary

To develop a successful government Web site that provides value to government procurement managers and to government vendors and buyers of government surplus and debt, developers of such sites have to do six things well:

1. Maintain extensive databases of up-to-date government procurement contact information and news.

2. Maintain extensive databases of vendors with references from past government purchasers about the quality of the vendors' service. This database should also provide information on the credit-worthiness of the vendor.

3. Allow government procurement managers to buy directly from the Internet from approved government vendors.

4. Assist in finding funding sources to help finance government contracts.

5. Assist in finding partners to work with on government contracts.

6. Make the site simple and easy to navigate.

Chapter 15
Future Predictions

THE MAJOR QUESTIONS THAT EVERYONE wants answers to—
whether they are investors, businesspeople, or consumers—include the
following:

- At what stage is the Internet in its life cycle?
- What business opportunities are still available?
- What are investors looking to invest in?
- Can companies succeed that enter the market after the leader?
- Will today's Internet corporate leaders dominate into the new millennium?
- Is the retail Internet market saturated?
- Will companies take to the Internet like consumers when making purchases?
- How much money will it take to build a successful Internet business?
- Will 100 percent of business purchases end up going through the Internet?
- What technologies will have the greatest impact?

Yesterday

Ten years ago I worked for Dr. Hubert J. P. Schoemaker, chairman of Centocor, one of the first biotechnology companies, when biotechnology stocks were as hot as Internet stocks. When I traveled with Dr. Schoemaker, it was like traveling with the business equivalent of a rock star. Everyone wanted his time and hung on his every word. His stock went from $10 a share to over $100 per share. His company, along with a few others, didn't receive Federal Drug Administration approval for certain "blockbuster" drugs. Therefore, its stocks dropped and all of the money that was being thrown at it disappeared.

As quickly as Wall Street promoted biotechnology stocks as the next great way to make a lot of money, it was just as quick to demand revenue and profits from these companies before they had time to fully develop and attain government approvals to sell their drugs. Stocks like Centocor and brilliant entrepreneurs like Dr. Schoemaker were snickered at. Although Centocor's stock never climbed back into the hundreds of dollars, it did manage to go from $5 to the mid-$50s before being bought by Johnson & Johnson for a few billion dollars.

Today

The Internet has reached the weeding-out stage in its life cycle, where only the best concepts that generate revenue without giving away products and services at a loss survive. Between July and November of 2000, more than 240 dot.com companies went bankrupt, and 22,000 people lost their jobs. Such high-flying companies as Internet Capital Group, Yahoo!, CMGI, Amazon.com, and others saw their share prices drop by an average of 80 percent. By the time you read this book, I am sure the casualty list will have grown.

The big difference between biotechnology and the Internet is that it takes ten years or more for a biotechnology company to develop and get a drug approved before it can even begin to bring in revenues, whereas an Internet business can start generating revenue almost immediately. In biotechnology, there can be only a limited number of winners because there are only a certain number of maladies to develop drugs for. The cost of starting a biotechnology company is in the millions, and to see it through to the revenue stage costs hundreds of millions of dollars.

Anyone with a computer can start an Internet company. Due to the myriad software development tools that nontechnical people can use to develop their own sites, the cost of development is shrinking and the road to profitability is shorter. Within two years, I would bet that every home will have an Internet connection and everyone will have an e-mail address just as they have a telephone number and now a mobile telephone number.

The future mobile telephone will allow you to buy products and services and respond to e-mails. Profitability for many of these mobile telephone companies will take less time than people think because the price of mobile telephones and mobile service is coming down, which means more people can afford it. Even in countries like Panama, where the average professional makes around $10,000 a year, everyone is walking around with a cell phone.

Tomorrow

This chapter will contain the views of one of the leading Internet analysts on Wall Street, Charles Phillips, and one of the world's leading Internet investors and Internet billionaires, Doug Alexander, president of Internet Capital Group Europe. The last view of the future will be from the author of this book.

Interview with Charles Phillips

Charles "Chuck" Phillips is a managing director and one of Wall Street's top analysts. Phillips joined Morgan Stanley Dean Witter in

December 1994 as an equity research analyst covering enterprise software companies. He has been covering the enterprise software sector since 1986. Prior to Morgan Stanley Dean Witter, he covered these stocks for Kidder Peabody, SoundView Financial, and The Bank of New York. He is ranked the number one industry analyst in enterprise/server software by Institutional Investor magazine and has been a member of their All-America research team every year since 1994. Phillips received a BS in computer science from the U.S. Air Force Academy, after which he served as a captain in the Marine Corps, working in the data processing field. He earned an MBA in finance from Hampton University in Virginia, and a JD from New York Law School. Phillips is a member of the Georgia State Bar and is a chartered financial analyst.

What is the ideal B2C opportunity?

The ideal B2C business model features the following elements:

- Small purchase size
- Network effect
- Two constituents per transaction
- Payment by credit card
- Negotiation is not common/wanted
- Limited customer relationship/integration leads to low switching costs and customer retention
- Impulse buy more likely
- Brand name important

What is the ideal B2B opportunity?

The ideal B2B model focuses on the following:

- Low concentration of buyers
- High number of geographically dispersed suppliers

- High number of existing intermediaries
- High number of transactions per $1 million of trading volume
- Low touch, standard products
- High churn rate; high average number of repeat trades (e.g., stocks)
- Industry with few self-service options and low customer service levels
- Frequent excess capacity
- Unpredictable demand and therefore production needs
- Regional markets that could potentially go global
- Low brand name impact; product availability more important than seller's identity
- Volatile supplier/buyer relationships

What will it take to succeed in e-commerce?

I would say companies who think of processes and functions as opposed to point and time transactions. That is important. You need to develop reasons for users to come back to your site. You have to understand what the customer wants in terms of process and that will add more value.

Who does that well?

It hasn't played out yet, but those are the companies that will do well.

What does it take to succeed in the content area?

It depends on the content. There is no formula for that and who gets there first, and getting there first is more important in B2C than B2B. Brand names are harder to overcome in the B2C market.

How important is first mover advantage?

It is helpful in B2B, but doing it right is more important. Unlike consumers, who buy on impulse, businesses look at value.

How entrenched are the first movers in B2B?

No one is entrenched because no one has any meaningful revenues. First movers do have customer recognition, process, and an understanding of what the customer wants. Things can change pretty quickly when a few large buyers try to partner or buy from a particular company. That can change who will be the leader.

What are the smart companies doing?

They are actually going out and physically talking to the customers and finding out what functions need to be added.

How important is it to have a direct sales force?

Depending on the service, you are going to have to have some type of outbound calling effort. Running advertisements and direct mail are just not enough in most markets. You need people to physically go out and speak to the customer. You can't get around it.

What businesses will the Web affect the most?

Energy, plastics, telecommunications, chemicals, paper, and industries with complex processes and fragmented businesses like consulting and printing.

Industries with a small number of buyers and that are concentrated won't be successful. Industries like the aircraft industry, where the buyers and sellers are all known to each other.

What are the CEOs of the future going to look like?

They will be more technologically aware. You will see more CIOs become CEOs. The CEOs will be a lot more specialized.

What types of employees are companies in the future going to need?

I think the same types of people as they need now. They need to be smart and understand and be able to use technology. The way those employees are organized will be different. People will work like SWAT teams. They will work as teams and go from project to project. People will need to be able to work with multiple customers, and companies will be more organized to better utilize their in-house talent to service customers.

What has surprised you?

I don't think it has happened as quickly as I would have thought. The business process and relationships haven't happened as quickly as I thought. Some people are fighting change and don't want it to happen. It is a more gradual change.

What revenue sources won't be around for the long term?

All forms of revenue like banner advertisements will be around. I just think rates will go down. I think credit card fees will go down because they are too high and a lot less risk.

Interview with Douglas A. Alexander

Douglas A. Alexander has served as one of the managing directors of Internet Capital Group (ICG) since September 1997. Prior to joining ICG, Alexander cofounded Reality Online, Inc., in 1986 and sold it to Reuters Group in 1994. Alexander continued to serve as president and CEO of Reality Online after its acquisition by Reuters Group until September 1997 and was a key contributor to Reuter's Internet initiatives. Alexander is chairman of the board of VerticalNet, Inc., and serves as a director of Arbinet Communications, Inc.; Blackboard,

Inc.; ComputerJobs.com, Inc.; Deja.com, Inc.; eMerge Systems; LinkShare Corporation; SageMaker, Inc.; and StarCite.

What do you look for when you are investing?

We are looking for size of market opportunity. How are you are going to maximize opportunity? How will the business model maximize opportunity? This includes the revenue, the site's stickiness and management. We see a lot of B2B markets with enormous size but few profit prospects, and we look at small B2B opportunities with big profit possibility. It all depends on the model. There are two buckets you can and can't fix. We look at the structure of the industry and how the Internet will impact it. Then we look at the standard stuff—management and execution. A fragmented market with solid profit margins and a team that knows and has credibility in the industry has the greatest chance for success.

What will Internet companies look like over the next five years?

They will be bigger or they will be extinct. In general, there will be a lot of consolidation. You will see consolidation because of company acquisitions. Amazon.com and Yahoo! are doing this in the B2C area. You need to leverage customer acquisition.

B2B is totally different. There are many markets with billion-dollar opportunities. Our structure is to attack multiple markets. This allows for leveraging markets. You will see one dominant Internet player in each segment.

The number one player is going to be worth ten times the number two player. It is like when Microsoft started. There were five companies offering operating systems, and now there are only Microsoft and Apple, which only has a small piece of the pie.

What skill sets will management and employees need?

An insane and irrational sense of urgency! Management and employees need to adapt quickly because markets evolve quickly. You need to build a coherent vision that employees, customers, and investors understand and can support. You can't micromanage.

The founders/top executives have to be able to attract world-class people. There is a saying on the Internet: "the big don't eat the small, the fast eat the slow."

What is the part of the business company leaders underestimate?

They underestimate everything. That ranges from site building, competition, how much money it will take, the number of people. The biggest issue I found is that you need people with traditional business experience, but who move fast. You need the experience of a fifty-year-old and the energy of a twenty-five-year-old.

What stage in its life cycle is the Internet?

B2C is in the fifth inning, and B2B is in the top of the first.

How much money does it take to build a successful Internet company?

As the industry matures, the amount of money grows. In B2C it's $75 million, up from $5 million four years ago. Now companies are running Super Bowl ads. For B2B, you need $25 million and that number goes up as the amount of competitors grows. First mover is important because the first mover gets the publicity and attention from the media and the best-quality investors.

What technologies have the biggest impact?

Over the next several years, the biggest impact will come in the areas of non-PC access devices, wireless connectivity, and broadband.

Non-PC devices will be greater than PCs in terms of numbers.

Just follow a college student for a day. They don't look at the PC as a tool to do work. They look at it as an appliance like a refrigerator or a television. It gives them something they want and need. They look at it as a device that makes everything work. Most of us look at a newspaper for movie times, but a college student goes right to the Net to find out where and when a movie is playing.

What is the future of the Internet?

I believe Wall Street and individual investors descended on the Internet like hungry people rushing to a buffet table. They tasted the food, fell in love with it, and then they ate so much that it made them sick. Once everyone's stomach has settled down, you will see a renewed frenzy, but you probably won't see the stratosphere stock prices again. My view of life in the Internet is broken down into three areas, which are: business-to-consumer, B2B, and government-to-business-to-consumer.

Why will B2C rebound?

- Consumers have no emotional ties to those they buy from.
- Consumers are interested in who will give them the best price.
- Consumers are interested in who will give them the greatest variety.
- Consumers are interested in easy return policies.
- Consumers don't have layers of bureaucracy to go through to make a buying decision.
- Consumers will be able to go into a store online, speak to a sales assistant, and go from department to department because the use of video will be commonplace as the speed of video feeds becomes faster. The sales assistant may be real or may be animated. Go to *www.knoa.com* and download their free technology, and you will see how sales and customer service will be altered in the future.

- Consumers will be able to see 3-D models of themselves trying on clothes from their homes and will order clothes over the Internet without actually having to go to the store.
- Consumers will be called on their personal digital assistants or telephones about sales and discounts on items they are interested in.
- Consumers will purchase airline tickets and arrange for trips directly with the provider of those services. The travel agency business as it relates to consumers will go from selling transportation tickets and arranging vacation packages to providing third-party reports on experiences of other travelers by age, region, and economic status.
- Consumers in very small numbers will embrace buying groceries over the Internet. Investors will see that online grocery shopping is one area the Internet couldn't significantly affect.

What is the future of B2B?

B2B will be enormous, but it will take a lot longer than people think. Just look at Internet superstar VerticalNet's sales results related to the number of salespeople they have selling products and the number of sites they are operating. VerticalNet had slightly over $100 million in sales spread out over fifty-plus business verticals that were being sold by over 220 salespeople. That comes out to $400,000 a vertical and $160,000 per salesperson. I would bet on average the salespeople are making more than they are bringing in. The expectation in most industries is that a salesperson will sell a minimum of $1 million worth of product or service. The reasons adoption will take longer are as follows:

- Purchasers have relationships with sellers and those relationships won't be easily changed. How many times have you pitched to a prospective buyer a product or service that was better and cheaper than what he already had, but the buyer refused to change vendors because he had an established relationship with another vendor?

- Purchasers still want to meet with the people they are buying from in person. It's one thing to buy a commodity like a computer, and it's totally different to buy an expensive hard good such as a tractor.
- Banks haven't fully integrated with business Web sites to provide real-time online credit approval.

Because of competition and the need for speed, top management will be pushing purchasing managers to buy their products and services through the Internet. The reasons the B2B market will be huge are as follows:

- Purchasers will be able to go to one site like *www.rfpmarket.com* and put in a purchase order and have vendors bid on the opportunity. If it is a large corporation that spends billions of dollars and has a huge database of vendors, it will set up its own exchange. This is happening now through the use of software from *www.freemarkets* and *www.commerceone.com* and will continue to be a huge growth opportunity.
- Purchasers will be able to buy outside their regions and go to a site that aggregates all the sellers, which will allow buyers to put up their requests and get the best price.
- Sellers will be able to reduce their travel costs because buyers and sellers will speak to each other through improved video technology.
- Sellers that offer unique products and services will be able to join international and regional business markets.
- Companies will do most of their future training over the Internet, and people who work full time will pick up their advanced degrees without ever going onto a college campus.
- Products and supplies will be ordered automatically as items are

scanned through a barcode reader, transmitted electronically through the Internet, and sent to the manufacturer or distributor. For example, when the amount of supplies in a company's supply room gets below a certain level, an order will be placed to a business supplier like OfficeDepot.com, and the supplies will be automatically bought and delivered. The credit limits for purchasing the supplies will be agreed on in advance, and money will be automatically transferred.

What is the future of Government-to-Business-to-Consumer?

The Internet is quickly changing the way we interact with government. Companies and individuals are filing their taxes online at the federal and state levels and by the time you read this book many local governments will be accepting payment over the Internet. The Internal Revenue Service reported that consumers paid $9 billion in taxes through the Internet. Local municipalities and state governments see the Internet as a way to lower the cost of running government and enhancing public services.

The economy within five to ten years will be a true global marketplace because the Internet will eliminate all of the boundaries. The only major concern is how local, state, and federal governments will tax Internet businesses. Countries like the United States that develop the leading-edge technology, and states like California, Massachusetts, New York, New Jersey, Pennsylvania, Texas, and Washington that produce the leading Internet companies, could create such huge disparities in wealth that lesser countries and states will want to put some type of restrictions or controls on how people and companies buy products and services in order to protect their tax bases.

I don't know what the price of the stocks for Internet companies will be when this book comes out, but I am buying Internet stocks with a strong brand name, a good business model, and a lot of cash. I am willing to hold on until the stocks rebound. The stock market is just going through a cycle, but make no mistake, the Internet is here to stay and has and will continue to change the way we conduct business. Let me know what you think of this book and your views on the Internet by writing to me at *marc@kramercommunications.com* and I will post your thoughts on my Web site.

Appendix A:
Sample Business Plan

Spiritualgifts.com

Executive Summary

Spiritual Gifts, Inc., is one of the nation's largest and most profitable spiritual and multidenominational gift, book, and music retailers in the United States, with $25 million in sales. Spiritual Gifts is implementing a separate division so as to develop a position in international gifts through its new Web site called Spiritualgifts.com. Currently, Spiritual Gifts, located outside of Cincinnati, Ohio, sells its products to individual consumers through twenty-five stores in Ohio, Michigan, and Indiana and through a catalogue that is distributed to 50,000 people nationwide. The company's catalogue sales are $5 million.

Market Opportunity
Internet Growth

IDC, a marketing research firm, estimates that the number of Web users will grow from 70 million to approximately 320 million by 2002.

Americans are being driven to the Internet by affordability and Web ubiquity. The Yankee Group, a leading market research firm, found that personal computers are getting cheaper, and The Yankee Group reports that Internet access is the number one reason consumers are buying computers. Household PC penetration jumped from 43 to 49 percent between June and December of 1998, and household Internet penetration leapt to 37 percent in that time, according to Inteco. Inteco estimates that by the end of 2003, PC penetration in the United States will reach 65 percent and household Internet access will hit 58 percent.

According to Mediamark Research, 58 percent of online users are over the age of thirty-five, and 67 percent of the users have an income over $50,000.

PriceWaterhouse/Coopers, one of the Big Five accounting firms, stated in their 1998 technology report that by the year 2003, the number of households with an Internet connection will mirror that of telephones and that B2C sales will reach $500 billion.

Christian Market

The Christian community on the Internet represents one of the largest communities on the Web (estimated at 30 million adults in 1998 by USA Today/Barnes Research).

Sales in the religious and inspirational product category hit $4 billion in 1998, according to Inspirational Giftware magazine. The spiritual gift market, according to Inspirational Giftware, has grown over 40 percent in the past six years. According to a January 1, 1999, Christian Retail magazine article, 25 percent of Christian Internet-connected households were shopping on the Internet in 1998; and that number is expected to grow to 52 percent by 2002.

Jewish Community

There are 6 million Jews in the United States and they spend approximately $600 million a year on gifts, according to the Jewish

Federation. This market is expected to grow 20 percent per year over the next five years.

Buddhist Community

There are over 2 billion Buddhists worldwide, a following that exceeds every other religion. Buddhists are expected, according to International Dataquest, to spend $100 to $200 billion worldwide on gifts. As their income continues to grow, so will the amount they spend on gifts.

Internet Experience

In the fall of 1998, Spiritual Gifts, believing their in-store retail and catalogue experience was a perfect springboard into offering their products over the Internet, launched a basic Web site called *www.Favoritegifts.com*. Spiritual Gifts set no revenue goals. Their sole purpose was to test market the level of interest in Christian consumers buying spiritual gifts on the Internet. Through the use of Flycast, an online media buying company, Spiritual Gifts ran a few advertisements and found out that the market potential for selling spiritual gifts online far exceeded the opportunity to continue to build physical stores. Currently the average sale in the physical stores is $43 per customer versus the Web's $59 per customer, which is a per sale increase of 30 percent per customer.

During a six-week trial period, Spiritual Gifts ran national advertisements promoting Spiritualgifts.com. The site had over 2,000 visitors, of which over 850 spent an average of $59 per purchase. Mary James, president of Spiritual Gifts, firmly believes that with her family's extensive knowledge of Christian gift acquisition and direct marketing through catalogues, and with proper funding, a separate online spiritual gift company called Giftswithlove, Inc., would be a great success.

Strategy for Capturing Sales

Spiritualgifts.com will leverage Spiritual Gifts's national reputation and contacts to do the following to drive sales:

- Develop an "affiliates" program initially with 18,000 Catholic churches and then work with other Christian and non-Christian churches, organizations, schools, and hospitals.
- Develop an "affiliates" program with other religious content-oriented Web sites.
- License its mailing list of 50,000 qualified purchasers, which is updated three times a year.
- Utilize Spiritual GiftsShop's catalogue database of 50,000-plus gifts and inventory of 8,000 different gifts.
- Utilize Spiritual GiftsShop's secondary mailing list that includes 850,000 names.
- Utilize Spiritual GiftsShop's successful catalogue business to promote online site.

Minimizing Risk

Unlike many e-commerce startups in which the entrepreneurs have no experience in the field they are trying to dominate and don't already have a system in place, Spiritualgifts.com increases its chances for success because it has the following:

- Working warehouse and an established process for receiving and shipping goods.
- Gift returns on the Web site have been zero.
- Gift returns from the catalogue and in the store have been less than a tenth of 1 percent historically.
- Initially Spiritualgifts.com will outsource marketing, media buying, and IT development in order to keep overhead costs down and obtain experienced professionals to build the business.

Future Opportunities

There are five other opportunities we plan to go after over the next five years that are not reflected in our projections, and they are as follows:

1. 220,212 non-Catholic, English-speaking churches.
2. 2,517 Spanish-speaking churches (develop a Spanish language gift site).
3. 2,837 synagogues; we could be their online gift store.
4. 7,484 Catholic high schools; we could be their online gift store.
5. 6,203 museums; we could provide their online spiritual gifts.

Successfully entering these markets could double or triple our revenue forecasts.

Management

Management of Spiritualgifts.com has almost 100 years collectively of multidenominational retail, direct marketing, and management experience. The president of the new company is Mary James, who has grown Spiritual Gifts from $3 million to $25 million in four years. She and her three sisters will manage Spiritualgifts.com, and as the site continues to grow, they will integrate the management team with outsiders experienced in electronic commerce and Internet marketing.

Mission and Objectives

The mission of Spiritualgifts.com is to provide Christians in the Americas and Europe with access to the largest array of spiritual products that fit anyone's budget and to provide a safe shopping experience.

Short-Term Objectives: Years 1–2

- Generate sales of $20 million
- Develop a Hispanic version of Spiritualgifts.com

Summary Financial Projects

Revenue	Year 1	Year 2	Year 3	Year 4	Year 5
Participation fee	$—	$60,000	$132,000	$435,600	$1,437,480
Product sales	$3,600,000	$7,920,000	$17,424,000	$38,332,800	$84,332,160
Sponsorships	$48,000	$105,600	$232,320	$511,104	$1,124,429
Shipping revenue	$480,000	$1,056,000	$2,323,200	$5,111,040	$11,244,288
Total	$4,128,000	$9,141,600	$20,111,520	$44,390,544	$98,138,357
Total Expenses	$4,994,600	$9,303,335	$18,241,164	$36,575,440	$76,115,643
Profit/(loss)	($866,600)	($161,735)	$1,870,357	$7,815,104	$22,022,714

Long-Term Objectives: Years 3–5

- Generate sales of over $95 million
- Raise $20 million through a public offering
- Market products to all denominations

Company Background

Sam and Gene James started Spiritual Gifts in the existing first store in Cincinnati, Ohio, in 1965. They started by selling small religious articles to local parishes and now have expanded to six stores in two states. The Jameses have four daughters, and all of the children play a role in the business.

Gene James died in 1994. Prior to his death, he appointed his oldest daughter, Mary, as president of the company. Under Mary's leadership, the company has grown from $3 million to $25 million in sales, which translates into a 100 percent–plus growth rate.

Over the years, the company has expanded outside of retail to provide supplies and restoration to churches, synagogues, and religious schools around the country. The company began selling its products through a catalogue. Its catalogue business has grown to 50,000 subscribers and $5 million in business per year.

Market Opportunity
Growth of the Net

The household Internet penetration rate in the United States is at 25 percent, and should be close to 67 percent by the end of 2003, according to The Yankee Group (March 23, 1999). The Yankee Group reports that U.S. consumers will spend $56 billion on Internet access through ISPs over the next five years, and the market will grow at a compound annual rate of 21 percent over the same time period. By the end of 1999, approximately one-third of U.S. households will be online.

Electronic Commerce

Retail revenues generated from online shopping worldwide will increase by 784 percent over the next four years, from $4.5 billion by year-end 1998, to $35.3 billion by 2002, according to eMarketer's "eCommerce: Retail Shopping Report." The report states that online shopping will provide thousands of retailers with expanded revenue opportunities and new ways of reaching new customers and enhancing existing customer relationships.

The New Internet Users

Started using Net:	In past year	More than a year ago
Percent of all Net users	46	53
Percent of users who are:		
Male	48	55
Female	52	45
Age		
18–29	25	30
30–49	52	50
50–64	16	15
65+	4	4
Income		
$50,000+	35	45
$30,000–49,000	23	22
Under $30,000	23	16
Education		
College grad	29	46
Some college	32	30
HS grad	33	19
Less than HS	6	3
Use Net for		
Work	24	30
Pleasure	52	39
Mix	22	31

Source: Pew Research Center

Spiritual Gifts Market

The Family Christian Stores, a trade publication, reports that the market for Christian retail is $4 billion and growing at a rate of 9 percent per year. According to an article in the March 1999 issue of the leading Christian industry retail magazine, Inspirational Giftware, entitled "Online Stores Carve Internet Presence," market research firms Forrester Research and Cyber Dialogue report that consumer online spending in 1998 was $7.9 billion and gift spending was $1.9 billion. These numbers are expected to grow to $17 billion and $7 billion respectively by 2001. John Williams, CEO of the J.C. Williams Group, the third-largest retail consulting firm in the world, made the following observation at the Christian Business Association (CBA) Future conference on March 12–13, 1998, in Colorado Springs: "The Christian retail industry has an unprecedented opportunity to flourish in the coming years, due largely to the problem-oriented culture in America. Christian retailers are in the 'making a difference' industry, the solutions industry."

According to Inspirational Giftware magazine, the market for spiritual gifts is growing at a rapid rate because of the concerns Williams alluded to about society and one's happiness in a rapidly changing culture. The fastest-growing product category is stationery and gifts, representing $1.7 billion. As of the writing of this plan, there is no dominant electronic commerce site focused on selling spiritual gifts.

Site Content

In order to enrich the users' shopping experience and give the user the feeling that Spiritualgifts.com isn't just another gift site, Spiritualgifts.com will develop the following shopping service/support and experience:

Gift Club

First time users will be asked if they would like a free gift for visiting Spiritualgifts.com. First-time users will log on to the site by providing the following in exchange for a free gift:

- Name
- Address
- Telephone number
- E-mail address

Reminder Calendar

Once the information is entered, users will be offered an opportunity to fill out a Spiritualgifts.com Reminder Calendar. This calendar will send e-mail reminders ten and five days before special events such as birthdays and anniversaries. Users will be asked to plug in the names, addresses, and telephone numbers of people they would like on their gift list.

Shopping History

Users will be able to go to the site at any time to see what they bought for whom and when they bought it. If the user elects not to fill out the calendar, then the user will be sent directly to the site to shop.

Exposure Game

A game will be set up that requires users to visit the various sections of the site to increase exposure of the site, which will hopefully generate sales. Individuals who participate in the game will win a Spiritualgifts.com T-shirt.

Gift Ideas

An extensive list of gift categories, products, and gift suggestions will be found on the site.

- Birth
- Graduation
- Housewarming
- Mother's Day
- Pets
- Death
- Sports
- St. Patrick's Day
- Thank you
- Teachers

- Religious holidays
  (Christmas, Lent, Easter)
- Weddings
- Religious events (Baptism, Holy
  Communion, Confirmation)

Product categories

- Angels
- Art
- Books
- Candles
- Cards
- Clothing
- Collectibles
- Educational

- Ethnic
- Games
- Jewelry
- Music
- Statuary
- Video
- W.W.J.D.
- Youth

Intelligent Shopper Assistance

Oftentimes shoppers aren't sure what they want. Working with a New York Web site tools development company, the James family will provide an intelligent shopper that speaks to the user and assists the user in finding the appropriate gift. The shopper will be an animated icon character that will look like and have the voice of the founding matriarch of Spiritual Gifts, Mrs. James. The animated shopper will pull its knowledge from a database of shopping suggestions culled from the Jameses' quarter of a century of spiritual gift retail experience.

Using an animated shopper will give the site a more personal feel, and connecting that with an intelligent database will hopefully cut down the number of returned gifts to zero and limit the need to speak to a customer service representative.

Editorial Content

- Top ten gifts, books, and music.
- Funny gift-buying stories.

- Favorite gifts given and received by famous Christians. This would include Christian singers, clergy, and actors.

- Surveys—Spiritualgifts.com will run surveys with its users to determine what gifts people most like to receive for various occasions such as Mother's Day, Father's Day, Christmas, and Easter.

- A monthly column bylined by Mrs. James dealing with holidays, gift giving, and family stories related to the store. This could include a sound bite as well.

- "Ask Mrs. James" section where people can submit questions for gift suggestions and receive an e-mailed response. Over time, the answers will be automated because the collection of questions and responses developed for this section of the site will be stored in a database.

- History of the store and how it came to be.

- Return policy.

- Questions and answers about shopping on the site.

- Questions and answers about how independent manufacturers can sell their product through the site.

Customer Retention

Most products will be shown with a photograph, brief description, and price. Some items, such as books and videos, may not require photography. Music could include sound bites. In order to retain customers, Spiritualgifts.com will do the following:

- Initially partner with the 18,000 Catholic churches and over 50,000 non-Catholic churches nationwide to offer a 10 percent commission to the church each time a parishioner buys something from Spiritualgifts.com, or a 15 percent discount from Spiritual GiftsShop's church supply division.

- Develop a "specials" or "sale" section that would discount products that are out-of-season or not moving.

- Institute a frequent buyer program. For every $100 spent, Spiritualgifts.com will give buyers a $10 coupon to toward a future purchase, or money will be sent in their name to their place of worship.

- Develop value-added content for the site to encourage repeat visits and to position the James Family Spiritual GiftsShop as a true expert in the field.

- List traditional and contemporary anniversary gifts with products that fit the descriptions.

- Offer a bulletin board where people can post thanks and stories of religious experiences.

- Develop a series of online chats with notable individuals such as authors. This could be a natural extension of any in-store appearances by a celebrity.

- Write book, music, and movie reviews that are relevant to products being sold or in the market.

- Develop an e-newsletter that can keep visitors posted on product additions, sales, et cetera.

- Offer electronic cards that visitors can have sent to loved ones around key holidays or religious events.

- Develop a scrip program where churches, schools, and religious organizations register on the site and then anytime someone makes a purchase and identifies himself or herself as belonging to that organization, money is earmarked to go to it. Twice a year (or more frequently if desired) the organization would receive a check reflecting the total amount.

- Develop a loyalty program for church goods. This could consist of giving churches a code that would be included on each purchase order. Once churches spend a certain amount, they would automatically receive a discount on future sales.

- Develop a referral program that each time a customer buys from

Spiritualgifts.com and mentions that another customer referred him, the referring customer will receive a 10 percent commission. Once they reach $10 in commissions, a check will be sent.

- Offer a free Web site for churches, religious organizations, hospitals, and schools and be the outsourced online gift shop.

Marketing Spiritualgifts.com

- Develop a network of sites on which Spiritualgifts.com establishes reciprocal links or executes a syndicated selling technique where those sites get a small percentage of whatever sales are generated from their site traffic. An e-mail campaign could be developed to notify desired sites of the new program and to encourage them to enroll.
- Develop an online advertising campaign to generate traffic and sales.

Direct Mail

Spiritual Gifts has its own catalogue that is mailed to 50,000 homes. The catalogue mailing list is updated every four months, and households that have not purchased anything from the catalogue within a year are removed from the mailing list. Below are mailing numbers for each catalogue.

- Christmas—800,000
- Spring—600,000
- General gift catalog—100,000
- Communion catalog—100,000

Publications

Develop creative advertisements to drive traffic to the site to run in advertising and print ads (Christian Science Monitor, Christian News, etc.).

Destination Sites

- *www.crosswalk.com* (the leading Christian Web site with 150,000 members and 2 million-plus unique click-throughs each month)
- Include the URLs in all printed materials for the stores.

Preliminary Link Opportunities

Publications

- *www.envoymagazine.com* (Catholic Press)
- *www.catholicdigest.org* (insightful and humorous religious magazine)
- *www.familycircle.com* (online version of popular magazine)
- *www.catechist.com* (magazine for religious educators)
- *www.ncrpub.com/celebration* (parish worship preparation publication)
- *www.liturgical.com* (St. Mary publication)
- *www.catholicnews.com* (religious news)
- *www.cwnews.com* (independent Catholic world news)

Irish

- *www.knightsofequity.org* (National Irish-Catholic organization)
- *www.larksspirit.com* (Information for those that support "freedom with justice for Ireland")

Kids/Family

- *www.childrenspartnership.org* (national organization for needs of children)
- *www.netparents.org* (PSAs, etc., for children)
- *www.parentsoup.com* (family/parenting info)
- *www.lifeteen.org* (gets teens involved)
- *www.familyrosary.org/room.htm* (kid, teen, family, and general information)

Competition

There are numerous Web sites that offer religious and spiritual gifts, but none of them are the "Amazon.com" or "E*Trade.com" in this business space. None of the competitors has the combination of physical locations and catalogue business—which provides visibility, built-in customer base, and access to customer intelligence in terms of what products consumers are interested in purchasing—that Spiritualgifts.com does.

The following are the company's current competitors.

Leaflet Missal Company
Religious Articles Company

URL: *www.leafletmissal.com*

Target: Individuals and institutions (churches)

Tagline: None

Overview

- The home page displays a large graphic and scrollable text below. Navigational text links are listed to the left.

- A text link to a browser e-mail form allows for e-mail from the Web site.

- The site was last updated in May 1998.

- Both a counter and a Web tracker are present.

- Online shopping was available via a secure server; however, their license to use the shopping technology has apparently expired (a message appears online to that effect).

- Offline ordering is available through mail, fax, or phone. Visa, MasterCard, and Discover are accepted.

- A Saint of the Day is featured.

- Sells numerous decorative and institutional items of the following types and in the following categories: Books, Children's Corner, Crucifixes, 14kt Gold, Holy Water Fonts, Incense & Candles, Irish Items, Recordings, Inspirational, Rosaries, Seraphim Classics, Statues, Videos, Video Listing, WWJD.

Comments

- The shopping cart does not work at this time.
- The design is of standard frame construction. Very average looking.
- The graphics are nice but take time to download. Maybe too much time.

Parable Christian Stores

URL: *www.parable.com*
Target: Individual consumers, young consumers
Tagline: "America's Leading Christian Retailers"

Overview

- The homepage is professional and conveys information on many different topics in several columns and with photos.
- Contests for religious band concert tickets.
- Real Audio occasionally available to sample music for sale.
- They sell a variety of products such as books, music, gifts, videos, software, et cetera.
- A search engine exists for products.
- Online shopping is coming soon.
- A store locator helps you find a member store in your area.
- Fun kids' section has amusements like printable coloring book pages.
- E-mail through the browser is available.
- A newsletter will be mailed to you if you register.
- Testimonials exist.
- The site has been rated okay by Safe Surf, an independent rater of sites.
- Surfers can select a long-distance carrier, which donates 10 percent of the charges to a church.

Comments

- This site is the most sophisticated of all critiqued.
- Animated logo on splash page and professional design throughout.
- Once a customer enters the order form area, all other navigation tools are invalidated so that one cannot leave unless using the "back" button on the browser.

J.M.J. Products

URL: *www.totallycatholic.com*
Target: Individual consumers
Tagline: "Totally Catholic Stuff"

Overview

- Homepage has a green junglelike pattern and is scrollable with text links.
- Utilizes shopping cart technology but does not accept credit cards! Asks for "drafts" from user's bank in place of a check.
- Sells Catholic stampers, kid's crafts, crucifixes, rosaries, medals, books & tapes, fonts/icons, cards, statues, software, children's items, holy cards, and sacramental items.
- Offers Internet specials.
- Includes pages devoted to their banner ad service and their recommended vendors for Web design.
- Gift certificates available.

Comments

- Online commerce without the ability to use credit cards takes away a crucial convenience aspect.
- This site is a simple HTML page with a background texture, a chart, and some graphics placed in. It scrolls for many pages, which detracts from the design and from navigation.

Catholic Family Catalog

URL: *www.pray4usa.com*

Target: Individual consumers

Tagline: "The resource for your entire Catholic family product needs!"

Overview

- The Web site opens with a painting and a Psalm. It scrolls down to numerous links, some graphics, and a counter.
- Sells apologetics books, audio, and videos; art; Bibles; Catholic books, audio, and videos; children and young adults' books, videos, catechisms, games, toys; crucifixes and holy water; family stuff; home schooling and educational products; jewelry; Marian books, videos, and audio; music; Pope John Paul II books, videos, and software, et cetera; prolife and cultural issues books, videos, et cetera; saints books; T-shirts
- Printable, mailable/faxable order form and toll free number.
- E-mail can be sent through the browser from a text link.
- A links section exists to Catholic sites.
- The site includes critiques of the light rays in a scanned photograph. The light rays are seen to resemble religious figures.

Comments

- The printable form method is obviously not as convenient as an online option.
- This site contains simple HTML pages with links placed in and a background texture.
- The navigation and design are impaired by the necessity for scrolling.
- The photo with the light rays is an interesting digression.

The Catholic Shopper

URL: *www.catholicshopper.com*

Target: Individual consumers and institutions (churches)

Tagline: "Presenting more than 5,000 Catholic Products"

Overview

- The home page opens with an illustration and a simply illustrated cross. The graphic buttons on the left use a blue color that conspicuously does not match the blue background.
- Online shopping using shopping cart technology is available for use with MasterCard, Visa, and Discover. Phone and fax numbers are also available.
- Large graphics are used so the consumers can see products well.
- Sells audiotapes, baptism gifts, Bibles, books, candles, catechetical, Catholic resource directory, computer programs, crucifixes, door knockers, First Holy Communion products, framed devotional pictures, games, gifts, holiday gifts, holy water fonts, home schooling items, jewelry, kids' stuff, magazine subscriptions, miraculous medals, music cassettes and CDs, nun doll collection, patron saint medals, religious art, rosaries, scapulars, stained glass prayer items, stationery, statues, T-shirts, videos, and wall plates.
- Monthly specials on products.
- Contains a fairly extensive list of links to other Catholic sites and links to several search engines.
- Lists all of its suppliers and upcoming conferences.
- Contains a Mission Statement.
- Lists contact info but no link to browser e-mail.

Comments

- The graphics are huge and take awhile to download.
- The design does not look like a professional executed it.

Management

The management team has 100-plus years of retail and catalogue selling experience.

President: Mary James

After graduating from the University of Ohio in 1980 with a management/marketing degree, Mary received her certification as a Liturgical Consultant (I.F.R.A) from the American Institute of Architects. Mary cofounded the Inspirational Book Company in 1984, which was a highly successful niche book marketing company. In two short years she developed sales to over $3 million.

Since 1995, as president of Spiritual Gifts, she has continually built, led, and guided the business. In three and a half years, she has grown sales without the aid of outside capital.

Vice President of Operations: Sue James

Sue has twenty-four years of retail operations experience. She is responsible for the day-to-day running of the business, which includes the twenty-five stores and the catalogue business.

Vice President of Gift Acquisitions: Wanda James

Wanda has fifteen years of retail purchasing experience. She is responsible for retail and wholesale ordering and is responsible for the purchasing of 51,000 unique products per year.

Vice President of Sales: Roberta James

Roberta has sixteen years of wholesale and retail sales experience. She has worked on the gift selection for Spiritual Gifts's Web site and in the selection and sale of church supplies.

Chief Marketing Officer: Larry Hall

Larry has fourteen years of marketing and management experience. He is a former president of an Internet company, American Web, which developed Bank of America and Travel International's Web site, and was a partner at EasternWeb, the largest Internet consulting firm in the world.

Chief Financial Officer: Neal Braman

Neal has fifty years of retail accounting and auditing experience. He has been responsible for the accounting for Spiritual Gifts for twenty-five years. He oversees tax and audit reports.

Technology/Operations
Current Operating Status

Web Site Development and Maintenance

Spiritualgifts.com's prototype Web site was developed and is currently maintained by Virtu and the online transactional services are performed by Infoquest Technologies. Both of these companies will be replaced when the site is redeveloped.

Telephone Orders

Telephone orders are put into the system and a pick ticket is produced. "Pickers'" go through the stockroom and pull the items to fill each order. The orders are left in individual bins for the mailroom personnel.

Mailroom personnel release the orders. If the stockroom is out of a particular item, then the item is put on back order and usually the item can be sent within two to four weeks.

Web Orders

Presently Web orders are downloaded from the site and manually entered into the system the same as telephone orders. The system is designed for Web orders to be downloaded electronically and automatically create picking tickets and customer numbers.

Credit Card Order
After authorizing the order, the merchandise is shipped.

Future Status
Because Spiritualgifts.com is not a technology company, management plans to continue to outsource the development, hosting, and the transactional services. Management will hire internal content editors/Web masters who will continue to update the site. It will also continue to provide the order fulfillment and manage its own customer database because it has a great deal of expertise from its catalogue business.

Web Orders
The company will send e-mail confirmation in the future.

Client History
Customers will automatically know what they ordered, when they ordered, and to whom the items were shipped.

Current Technology in Place
Operating system: Unix SCO
Accounting system: Real World Backroom
Point of Sale: Counter Point
Computer system: Pentium II 450, 128 Megs of RAM
                            and 6 gig hard drive.
Credit Card Authorization: CES

Spritualgifts.com

Revenue	Year 1	Year 2	Year 3	Year 4	Year 5
Participation fee	$ -	$60,000	$132,000	$435,600	$1,437,480
Product sales	$3,600,000	$7,920,000	$17,424,000	$38,332,800	$84,332,160
Sponsorships	$48,000	$105,600	$232,320	$511,104	$1,124,429
Shipping revenue	$480,000	$1,056,000	$2,323,200	$5,111,040	$11,244,288
Total	$4,128,000	$9,141,600	$20,111,520	$44,390,544	$98,138,357

Expenses

Revenue	Year 1	Year 2	Year 3	Year 4	Year 5
Salaries	$560,000	$955,000	$1,809,250	$3,387,673	$6,495,995
Taxes & benefits	$212,800	$362,900	$687,515	$1,287,316	$2,468,478
Travel	$55,000	$95,000	$165,000	$295,000	$535,000
Telephone	$19,800	$37,800	$63,000	$106,200	$485,000
Telephone 800 service	$11,000	$22,000	$44,000	$88,000	$176,000
Rent/utilities	$25,000	$105,000	$210,000	$210,000	$607,753
Marketing support	$1,000,000	$1,700,000	$2,950,000	$5,225,000	$9,437,500
Business supplies	$5,000	$8,925	$16,538	$28,941	$51,659
Business equipment	$60,000	$104,000	$169,000	$263,640	$342,732
Internet connection	$12,000	$12,600	$13,230	$13,892	$14,586

Expenses, *continued*

Revenue	Year 1	Year 2	Year 3	Year 4	Year 5
Web site development	$500,000	$750,000	$900,000	$1,080,000	$1,296,000
Professional services	$50,000	$60,000	$72,000	$86,400	$103,680
Product sales cost	$1,890,000	$3,780,000	$8,316,000	$18,295,200	$40,249,440
Packaging	$168,000	$369,600	$813,120	$1,788,864	$3,935,501
List acquisition	$6,000	$6,600	$7,260	$7,986	$8,785
Shipping	$320,000	$704,000	$1,548,800	$3,407,360	$7,496,192
Warehousing	$0	$30,710	$51,091	$64,514	$95,679
Affiliates commission	$0	$79,200	$261,360	$766,656	$2,108,304
Miscellaneous	$100,000	$120,000	$144,000	$172,800	$207,360
Total Expenses	$4,994,600	$9,303,335	$18,241,164	$36,575,440	$76,115,643
Profit/(loss)	($866,600)	($161,735)	$1,870,357	$7,815,104	$22,022,714

Spritualgifts.com

Revenue	Year 1	Year 2	Year 3	Year 4	Year 5
Participation fee	0	$60,000	$132,000	$435,600	$1,437,480
No. of products	0	50	100	300	900
Cost per product	0	$1,200	$1,320	$1,452	$1,597
Product sales	$3,600,000	$7,920,000	$17,424,000	$38,332,800	$84,332,160

Spritualgifts.com, *continued*

Revenue	Year 1	Year 2	Year 3	Year 4	Year 5
No. of customers per year	20,000	40,000	80,000	160,000	320,000
Avg. sale per customer per yr.	180	198	218	240	264
Sponsorships	$48,000	$105,600	$232,320	$511,104	$1,124,429
No. of sponsors	4	8	16	32	64
Avg. price per sponsor	$12,000	$13,200	$14,520	$15,972	$17,569
Shipping revenue	$480,000	$1,056,000	$2,323,200	$5,111,040	$11,244,288
No. of customers	20,000	40,000	80,000	160,000	320,000
No. of shipments	4	4	4	4	4
Charge per shipments	$6	$7	$7	$8	$9

Expenses

Revenue	Year 1	Year 2	Year 3	Year 4	Year 5
Management salaries	$255,000	$280,500	$308,550	$339,405	$373,346
President	1	1	1	1	1
Annual salary	$75,000	$82,500	$90,750	$99,825	$109,808
VP of operations	1	1	1	1	1
Annual salary	$70,000	$77,000	$84,700	$93,170	$102,487

Expenses, *continued*

Revenue	Year 1	Year 2	Year 3	Year 4	Year 5
VP of marketing	1	1	1	1	1
Annual salary	$70,000	$77,000	$84,700	$93,170	$102,487
VP of finance	1	1	1	1	1
Annual salary	$40,000	$44,000	$48,400	$53,240	$58,564
Administrative	$30,000	$63,000	$69,300	$152,460	$167,706
Annual salary	$30,000	$31,500	$34,650	$38,115	$41,927
No. of adminstrators	1	2	2	4	4
Warehouse personnel	$150,000	$315,000	$693,000	$1,524,600	$3,354,120
Annual salary	$25,000	$26,250	$28,875	$31,763	$34,939
No. of warehouse people	6	12	24	48	96
Client service	$100,000	$210,000	$441,000	$926,100	$1,944,810
Annual salary	$25,000	$26,250	$27,563	$28,941	$30,388
No. of client service people	4	8	16	32	64
Web site personnel	$25,000	$86,500	$297,400	$445,108	$656,013
Content coordinators	1	2	4	4	4
Annual salary	$25,000	$27,500	$30,250	$33,275	$36,603
Programmers	0	0	2	4	6
Annual salary	0	0	$55,125	$60,638	$66,701

Expenses, *continued*

Revenue	Year 1	Year 2	Year 3	Year 4	Year 5
Clerical assistance	0	1	2	2	3
Annual salary	$30,000	$31,500	$33,075	$34,729	$36,465
Taxes & benefits (% salary)	38%	38%	38%	38%	38%
Travel (per person per yr)	$5,000	$5,000	$5,000	$5,000	$5,000
Telephone (per person per yr)	$1,800	$1,800	$1,800	$1,800	$5,000
Telephone 800 service	$11,000	$22,000	$44,000	$88,000	$176,000
No. of calls	10,000	20,000	40,000	80,000	160,000
Cost per call	$0.11	$0.11	$0.11	$0.11	$0.11
No. of minutes per call	10.00	10.00	10.00	10.00	10.00
Rent/utilities	0	$180,000	$270,000	$270,000	$270,000
square feet	20,000	20,000	30,000	30,000	30,000
cost per sq foot	0	$9	$9	$9	$9
Marketing support	$1,000,000	$1,700,000	$2,950,000	$5,225,000	$9,437,500
Cable television	$400,000	$600,000	$900,000	$1,350,000	$2,025,000
Newspapers	$200,000	$300,000	$450,000	$675,000	$1,012,500
Direct mail	$100,000	$200,000	$400,000	$800,000	$1,600,000
Magazine	$200,000	$400,000	$800,000	$1,600,000	$3,200,000

Expenses, *continued*

Revenue	Year 1	Year 2	Year 3	Year 4	Year 5
Radio	$100,000	$200,000	$400,000	$800,000	$1,600,000
Business supplies (per person per yr)	$500	$525	$551	$579	$608
Business equipment (per person per yr)	$10,000	$13,000	$16,900	$21,970	$28,561
Internet consultants	$12,000	$12,600	$13,230	$13,892	$14,586
Web site development	$500,000	$750,000	$900,000	$1,080,000	$1,296,000
Professional services (legal, accounting)	$50,000	$60,000	$72,000	$86,400	$103,680
Product costs	$1,890,000	$3,780,000	$8,316,000	$18,295,200	$40,249,440
No. of customers per year	20,000	40,000	80,000	160,000	320,000
Cost per product sale	$90	$95	$104	$114	$126
Spiritual Giftscharge	1	0	0	0	0
Packaging	168,000	369,600	813,120	1,788,864	3,935,500
No. of boxes	84,000	168,000	336,000	672,000	1,344,000
Avg. cost per box	$2	$2.2	$2.4	$2.7	$2.9
List acquisition	$6,000	$6,600	$7,260	$7,986	$8,785
No. of lists	10	10	10	10	10
Cost per acquisition	$600	$660.0	$726.0	$798.6	$878.5

Expenses, *continued*

Revenue	Year 1	Year 2	Year 3	Year 4	Year 5
Shipping expense	$320,000	$704,000	$1,548,800	$3,407,360	$7,496,192
No. of customers	20,000	40,000	80,000	160,000	320,000
No. of packages	4	4	4	4	4
Charge per package	$4	$4	$5	$5	$6
Warehouse equipment	0	$30,710	$51,091	$64,514	$95,679
No. of shelves	0	20.0	26.0	33.8	43.9
Cost per shelf	0	$1,000	$1,100	$1,210	$1,331
Number of forklifts	0	1	2	2	3
Annual forklift rental	$10,200	$10,710	$11,246	$11,808	$12,398
Credit card fees	$63,720	$140,184	$308,405	$678,491	$1,492,679
Sales	$3,600,000	$7,920,000	$17,424,000	$38,332,800	$84,332,160
Fee	$0.0177	$0.0177	$0.0177	$0.0177	$0.0177
Affiliates commission	0	$79,200	$261,360	$766,656	$2,108,304
Sales	$3,600,000	$7,920,000	$17,424,000	$38,332,800	$84,332,160
Affiliate commission rate	10%	10%	10%	10%	10%
Percentage of sales from affiliates	0	10%	15%	20%	25%
Miscellaneous	$100,000	$120,000	$144,000	$172,800	$207,360

Notes

Income

- **Participation fee.** This is a fee for individuals who have created new products and would like Spiritualgifts.com to sell their products on their site.
- **Product sales.** Based on bricks-and-mortar traditional charges.
- **Sponsorships.** There are travel, banking, and other types of B2C marketing companies that will want to target this market and promote themselves on sites that drives a lot of traffic.
- **Shipping revenue.** There will be a markup on shipping.

Expenses

- **Management salaries.** Based on figures supplied by executive recruiting firms on what startup Internet companies are paying on average.
- **Taxes and benefits.** Based on a Price Waterhouse Coopers study on what companies pay on average to employees.
- **Travel.** Based on figures supplied by AAA.
- **Telephone.** Based on figures supplied by public relations department of Bell Atlantic.
- **Telephone 800 service.** Based on figures provided by AT&T small business services.
- **Rent and utilities.** Based on figures supplied by Building Owners and Managers Association.
- **Direct mail.** Based on figures provided by Direct Marketing Association.
- **Magazine ads.** Based on reviewing advertising press kits.
- **Public relations.** Based on contacting small and medium-sized public relations firms.
- **Business supplies.** Based on figures supplied by Staples public relations department.
- **Business equipment.** Based on figures supplied by Staples public

relations department.

- **Technology hosting.** Based on speaking with Digger and Bee.Net.

- **Professional services.** Based on contacting professional service firms.

- **Business insurance.** Based on figures supplied by New England Financial.

Index

A

Acquisition costs, xi, xii

Active X, 25

Advertising
  banner, 35–36, 120, 184, 198, 221
  broadcast media, 36–37
  direct mail, 37–38
  e-mail, 38
  event sponsorship, 38–39
  free content, 39
  integrated, 184
  online, 144–45
  print, 40–41
  trade show, 41

Advisory boards, 33

Affiliates, 35, 138–39, 151, 156, 197, 200

Alexander, Douglas A., 217, 221

Applications
  cost of, 79
  custom vs. off-the-shelf, 26–27, 57–58, 63
  developer experience with, 56–57, 62
  hosting service, 14
  integration of, 84, 93

Assumptions, testing, 4–5

B

B2B exchange sites, 159–70
  benefits of, 159–60
  capital for, 162, 170
  competition and, 161
  credit and, 164
  customer service, 163
  examples, successful, 164–68
  executives for, 162, 169
  first mover advantage, 162, 167
  interview, VerticalNet, 165–68

killers of, 160–61
media awareness and, 162
number of, 164
power of, 159–60
price/quality and, 161
proposals for, 161
quality of, 163–64
search engines and, 163
security, 163
success factors, 160, 161–64,
 167
summary of, 169–70
technologies, 168
transaction trails for, 163
user retention, 168
win-win approach to,
 162–63, 170
B2B sites
 B2C vs., 25–26
 cost of, 223
 future of, 225–27
 ideal opportunity, 218–19
 purchasing volume, xi
B2C sites
 B2B vs., 25–26
 cost of, 223
 future of, 224–25
 ideal opportunity, 218
 purchasing volume, xi
Banking sites (B2B), 171
Banner advertising, 35–36, 120,
 184, 198, 221
Bauman, David, 180
Bee.net, 67–71, 76–78
Billing mechanisms, 26

Billings, Hilary, 103, 109
Bizlaunch, xiii
Boxerjam, 144, 148–54
Brand awareness, 83
Bricks and mortar, 1–2
Broadcast media advertising,
 36–37
Business description, 6
Business plans, 1–10
 drafting, 8–9
 goal/functions of, 5
 pure dot.com, 3–9
 questions for, 2–3, 4
 realistic, 5
 samples, 9–10, 229–60
 sections of, 5–8
 summary of, 10
 testing assumptions for, 4–5
 traditional company, 1–3
Business sectors, 187–88
Business services/product sites,
 187–202
 categories of, 188–89
 delivery speed and, 189–90
 examples, successful,
 191–202
 first mover advantage, 200
 future of, 198, 202
 interactivity and, 190
 interview, iPrint.com,
 193–98
 interview, Office Depot,
 198–202
 news from, 191
 office supplies, 188

partnerships and, 197
price of, 195–96
products/pricing, 190, 191
sales leads from, 190–91
search engines and, 191
sector percents, 187–88
shipment tracking, 190
success factors, 189–91, 195,
   196, 200
summary of, 202
technologies, 197, 201
user retention, 197, 201
Business-to-business. *See* B2B
   sites
Business-to-customer. *See* B2C
   sites
Butler, Keith, 198

C

Cable access, 97, 147–48
Capacity planning, 29
Career sites. *See* Human
   resource service sites
Christensen, Burke A., 118
Christman, Ward, 136–38
C language, 84
Client service objectives, 82–83
Collocation, 77
Company objectives, 6
Competition, 7, 161
Confirmation capability, x
Consultants. *See* Developers
Content, site, 16, 85–86
Content-oriented sites
   hosting budgets, 78

success factors, 219
technical issues, 23–24
Costs
   acquisition, xi, xii
   application, 79
   hardware, 78
   maintenance, xiii, 134,
      209–10
   personnel, 79
   reducing, 97
   software, 79
   See also Prices, site
Credit cards, xi, 26
Cunningham, Allen A., 149
Custom applications, 26–27,
   57–58
Customers
   cost of, xi, xii
   executives and, 91–92
   feedback, 86–92
   needs, 83–84, 92–93
   prospective pool, xi, 97–98
   understanding, 32
   See also Users
Customer support, xiv
   B2B exchange site, 163
   content checklist for, 85–86
   financial services (B2C),
      119, 123, 124, 125
   management and, 91–92
   retail gift site, 97, 99, 100,
      110

D

Demographic data, 90, 146

Destination sites, 184
Developers
  application technology and,
    57–58, 63
  cost of, 58–60, 63
  criterion for, 13–14
  experience/location of,
    56–57, 62
  project manager for, 54–56,
    62
  prospective list, 13–14
  quality assurance and, 60–62,
    63
  scoping fees of, 53–54, 62
Development costs, xi
  controlling, example, 59–60,
    63
  host pricing sample, 68–71
  planning for, 27–28
  scoping fees, 53–54, 62
  See also Prices, site
Development testing, 136
DHTML, 140
Direct e-mail advertising, 38
Direct mail advertising, 37–38
Domain registration, 188

E

E-commerce sites
  failure causes, 87–88
  future of, 219
  hosting budgets for, 77–78
  hosting proposals, 66–67
  market research and, 86–92
  scalability, 25
  security, 24–25
  shopping carts and, 88–89
  technical issues, 24–25
  transaction integrity, 24
EdgarOnline, 205, 206–12
E-mail
  advertising, 38
  alerts, 173–74
  for B2B financial services,
    173–74
  boxes required, 79
  price list sample, 69
Employment sites. See Human
  resource service sites
Entertainment sites, 143–58
  advertiser value, 144–45
  cable access and, 147–48
  content creativity, 145
  demographic data and, 146
  download speed, 146
  examples, successful, 147–57
  excitement and, 145
  first mover advantage, 151,
    156
  future of, 154, 157
  graphics, 145–46
  interactivity and, 149, 158
  interview, Boxerjam, 149–54
  interview, Webstakes.com,
    154–57
  marketing, 149, 151–53, 156,
    157
  newsletters, 146–47
  number of, 143
  partnerships and, 147, 151

success factors, 145–47, 149–51, 154
summary of, 158
technologies, 153, 157
user equipment and, 147
user retention, 152, 156
value of, 144–45
Entrepreneurial advice, 130
Equity, external, 9
Event sponsorship, 38–39
Executive coaching, 130–31
Executives
customer relations and, 91–92
profiles of, 220, 223
Executive summaries, 6
Extranets, 26

F

Failure causes, 29, 87–88
Farros, Royal, 193
Feedback, customer, 86–92
Financial management, xiii
cost reductions, 97
plan for, 7–9
See also Development costs
Financial ratios, 9
Financial services (B2B) sites, 171–85
calendars, 174
community for, 185
customization of, 174
databases for, 172
e-mail alerts, 173–74
examples, successful, 174–84

first mover advantage, 178–79, 182
information flows and, 173
interactivity and, 173
marketing budget outlook, 182
newsletters, 174
online meetings for, 173
price of, 178, 180–82
skills for, 183
success factors, 172–74, 178, 182
summary of, 185
technologies, 179, 183–84, 185
types of, 171–72
user retention, 179, 183, 184
Financial services (B2C) sites, 111–26
content of, 113
customer relations, 119, 123, 124, 125
design factors, 122
elements of, 112–15
examples, successful, 115–24
first mover advantage, 118
functionality of, 114–15
future of, 124
human interaction, 114
interview, Quotesmith.com, 116–20
interview, Raging Bull, 120–24
marketing factors, 123
number of, 112

overview of, 111–12
partnerships and, 119
products, 113, 114, 125
purchases from, 113, 114
research services, 113
security, 115
success factors, 118, 122
summary of, 125–26
technologies, 119–20,
  123–24, 125–26
user retention, 119
First mover advantage
B2B exchange site, 162, 167
business services/products,
  200
entertainment site, 151, 156
financial services (B2B),
  178–79, 182
financial services (B2C), 118
future of, 219–20
government commerce site,
  211
human resource site, 135, 138
retail gift site, 103, 106
Free content advertising, 39
Future predictions, 215–28
B2B, 218–19, 225–27
B2C, 218, 224–25
business services/products,
  198, 202
capital requirements, 223
company profile, 222
destination site, 184
e-commerce, 219
entertainment site, 154, 157

executive profile, 220, 223
financial services (B2C), 124
first mover advantage, 219–20
government commerce, 212,
  227–28
Internet lifecycle, 223
investment prospects, 222
past history and, 216
personnel, 221, 223
questions for, 215
retail gift site, 108–9
sector impact, 220
technology, 223–24
today and, 216–17

G

Gift support, 99, 110
Government commerce sites,
  203–13
advertising revenue, 212
calendars, 205
databases, 205
directories, 205
education, 205
example, successful, 206–12
financing for, 205
first mover advantage, 211
future of, 212, 227–28
interactivity and, 205–6
interview, EdgarOnline,
  207–12
marketing factors, 211
news updates, 206
opportunities, 206
overview of, 203–4

price of, 209–10
ratings, 206
strategies, 206
success factors, 204–6, 209, 210
summary of, 213
types of, 203–4
user retention, 211–12
Granular security, 26

H

Hamlin, Steve, 106, 108
Hardware
costs, 78
hosting service, 14
ownership of, 66
servers, 77, 78
Hemsworth, Willard L., II, 116–18
High-speed cable access, 147–48
Hosting proposals, 66–76
evaluating, 74–75
price list sample, 68–71
questions for, 66–67
request for, 66–67
sample, 72–74
visiting sites and, 75–76
Hosting services, 65–79
budgets for, 77–78
capacity planning and, 29
collocation and, 77
evaluating, 14–15, 74–76
hardware, 14
in-house, 28–29, 66, 76–78
mirrored, 14–15, 77

outsourcing, 28–29, 66–76, 78
prospective list, 14–15
references for, 75
sample price list, 68–71
site size and, 66, 78
software, 14
technical support, 15
HTML, 16, 65
Human interaction, 99–100, 114
Human resource service sites, 127–41, 131–32
career advice and, 128, 129–30
cost of, 134
employee presentation and, 129
examples, successful, 131–40
executive coaching and, 130–31
first mover advantage, 135, 138
interactivity and, 129, 130–31, 141
interview, JOBNET.com, 136–40
interview, Right Management, 129–30, 134–36
job fairs and, 129
keys to, 128–31
networking on, 130
number of, 127
overview of, 127–28
partnerships and, 139
price of, 134
resumes and, 129, 141

salary surveys on, 130
success factors, 135, 138
summary of, 141
user retention, 135, 139–40

I
Informative, Inc., 87–92
In-house hosting, 66, 76–78
Integration, systems, 84, 93
Interactivity
  business services/product
    site, 190
  entertainment site, 149, 158
  financial services (B2B), 173
  government commerce site,
    205–6
  human resource service sites
    and, 129, 130–31, 141
Interface personnel, 28
International Communications
  Research, 187
Internet.com, 112
Internet use, xi, 97–98, 187–88
Internet World, 83
Intranets, 26
Investment sites (B2B), 172
Investorforce.com, xiii, 171,
  173, 175–80
Investors, 9
iPrint.com, 192–98
iQVC, 101, 104–8

J
Java, 25, 153
Job fairs online, 129

JOBNET.com, 131–32, 136–40
Jobs sites. *See* Human resource
  service sites

K
Killeen, Stephen J., 120

L
Launch plan, 7
Letts, Jim, 23
Lifecycle, Internet, 223
Link management, 23
Localization, 24

M
Maintenance costs, xiii, 134,
  209–10
Management
  creative/sensible, xiii–xiv
  customer feedback and, 86–92
  developer interface, 28
  executive profiles, 220, 223
  plan, 7, 8
  structure pitfall, 2
  See also Personnel
Mann, Paul, 87
Margins, xii
Marketing
  public relations and, 34
  research, 86–92, 149, 220
  sales strategy and, 7, 8, 9, 220
  strategies, 6–7, 8, 9
  surveys, 33
  tactics, 33–41
Marketing budgets, 138, 182

Marketing plans, 31–52
  advisory board for, 33
  audience and, 32
  keys to, 32–33
  media selection and, 32–33
  reason for, 31–32
  sample, 41–51
  summary of, 52
  surveys for, 33
  weapons for, 33–41
  See also Advertising
Media selection, 32–33
Mickelson, Robin, 134
Microsoft Office, 8
Mirrored hosting, 14–15, 77
Mission, 15

N
Name recognition, 83
Niches, xiii

O
Objectives, 6, 82–83
Office Depot, 191, 192–93,
  198–202
Office supplies, 188
Off-the-shelf applications,
  26–27, 57–58, 63

P
Partnerships, 39–40, 119, 139,
  147, 151, 197
Personnel
  costs, 79
  developer interface, 28

financial service (B2B), 183
future, 221, 223
retail gift site, 103–4, 107
retaining, 107, 119, 136, 140,
  152, 167
See also Management
Phillips, Charles, 159, 217–18
Plan A, 8
Plans, Web site. *See* Web site
  plans
Plan Write, 8
Predictions. *See* Future predictions
Prices, site, 58–60, 63
  business services/products,
    195–96
  financial services (B2B),
    178, 180–82
  government commerce,
    209–10
  human resource, 134
Print advertising, 40–41
Products
  availability of, 99, 190
  business site, 190, 191
  cross-selling, 114
  delivery of, 99
  financial services (B2C),
    113, 114
  free, 191
  retail gift, 97, 99, 100, 109
  return policies, 100, 109
  selection, 100, 109
  support, 100
Project managers, 54–56, 62

Proposals. *See* Hosting proposals; Web site proposals
Public relations, 34

Q

Quality assurance (QA), 29
  B2B exchange site, 163
  example, 61–62
  process, 60–62, 63
Questions for success, 2–3, 4
Quotesmith.com, 115–20

R

Raging Bull, 115–16, 120–24
Red Envelope Gifts Online, 101–4
Repeat users, xiii
Resumes, 129
Retail gift sites, 95–110
  cost reductions, 97
  customer base, 97–98
  customer relations, 97, 99, 100, 110
  elements of, 98–100
  examples, successful, 100–108
  first mover advantage of, 103, 106
  functionality of, 98, 109
  future prediction, 108–9
  gift support, 99, 110
  human interaction, 99–100
  interview, iQVC, 104–8
  interview, Red Envelope, 103–4
  price reductions, 96–97

  products, 97, 99, 100, 109
  return policies, 100, 109
  security, 98–99
  skills for, 103–4, 107
  success factors, 96–98, 103, 106
  technologies, 104, 108
  time savings with, 96
  uniqueness of, 104, 107
  user retention, 103, 107
Revenue streams, 7, 82
Right Management Consultants, 128, 129–30, 131–36

S

Salary surveys, 130
Sales leads, 190–91
Sales strategy, 7, 8, 9, 220
Sales volume, xii
Scalability, 25
Schoemaker, Dr. Hubert J. P., 216
Search engines, 163, 191
Security, x–xi
  B2B exchange site, 163
  e-commerce, 24–25
  financial services (B2C), 115
  granular, 26
  hosting, 66, 79
  in-house hosting for, 76–78
  retail gift site, 98–99
  target platforms and, 25–26
Servers, 77, 78
Shipment tracking, 190

Shopping carts, 88–89

Site management. *See* Hosting services

Site maps, 17

Size, site, 66, 78

Software. *See* Applications

Speed
  download, 97, 146
  High-speed cable access, 147–48
  order delivery, 189–90

Stokes, Unity, 154

Strategic objectives
  client service, 82–83
  revenue, 82
  user, 82
  visibility building, 83

Strausberg, Susan, 207

Success
  characteristics of, xii–xiv
  customer feedback and, 86–92
  planning for, 81–82
  questions for, 2–3, 4
  site content checklist for, 85–86
  strategic objectives for, 82–83
  technical functionality for, 83–85
  See also specific site types

Surveys, 33

Systems integration, 84, 93

T

Target platforms, 25–26

Team location, 56, 62

Technical issues
  billing mechanism, 26
  content-oriented site, 23–24
  e-commerce site, 24–25
  external integration, 84, 93
  failure causes, 29, 87–88
  hosting questions, 66–67
  internal management, 84, 93
  IS ownership of, 85
  link management, 23
  localization, 24
  scalability, 25
  target platform, 25–26
  transaction integrity, 24
  version control, 23–24
  work flow, 24
  See also Security

Technical support, 15, 29

Technology
  developer experience with, 57–58, 63
  future of, 223–24
  internal, 16
  plans, 83–85, 93
  revolutionary, 123–24
  site, 16

Testing, development, 136

Testing assumptions, 4–5

Thoms, William V., 116

Trade shows, 41

Training sites. *See* Human resource service sites

Transaction integrity, 24

Transaction trails, 163

U

Unique offerings, xii
Unix, 84
User retention, 7
  B2B exchange site, 168
  business services/products,
    197, 201
  entertainment site, 152, 156
  financial services (B2B),
    179, 183, 184
  financial services (B2C), 119
  government commerce site,
    211–12
  human resource site, 135,
    139–40
  retail gift site, 103, 107
Users
  description of, 16
  number of, 66, 78
  repeat, xiii
  strategic objectives for, 82
  See also Customers

V

Vcall, 171, 173, 180–84
Version control, 23–24
VerticalNet, 164–68
Visibility building, 83

W

Wahl, Colin, 176
Webopedia.com, 112
Web site hosting. *See* Hosting
  proposals; Hosting services
Web site plans, 11–30

  advice on, 23–29
  applications and, 26–27,
    57–58, 62–63, 79, 84
  B2B vs.B2C, 25–26
  content-oriented, 23–24
  criterion, 13–14
  developer list, 13–14
  development steps, 11–14
  e-commerce, 24–25
  hosting prospect list, 14–15
  long-term, 27
  site leader and, 12
  summary of, 29–30
  See also Technical issues
Web site proposals
  elements of, 15–17
  mission and, 15
  request for, 12
  sample, 17–22
Webstakes.com, 144, 148,
  154–57
Wetherell, Russ, 76
Wireless access, x
Work Flow, 24

X

XML, 16, 140